Cinzia White

The Storyteller's
SAMPLER QUILT

   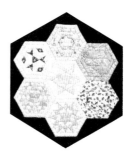 

Stitch 359 Blocks to Tell Your Tale

C&T PUBLISHING

Text and artwork copyright © 2019 by Cinzia White

Photography and artwork copyright © 2019 by C&T Publishing, Inc.

Publisher: Amy Marson

Creative Director: Gailen Runge

Acquisitions Editor: Roxane Cerda

Managing Editor: Liz Aneloski

Editors: Katie Van Amburg and Liz Aneloski

Technical Editor: Helen Frost

Cover/Book Designer: April Mostek

Production Coordinator: Tim Manibusan

Production Editor: Alice Mace Nakanishi

Illustrator: Cinzia White

Photo Assistant: Rachel Holmes

Photography by Kelly Burgoyne of C&T Publishing, Inc.,
unless otherwise noted

Published by C&T Publishing, Inc., P.O. Box 1456, Lafayette, CA 94549

Library of Congress Cataloging-in-Publication Data

Names: White, Cinzia, 1958- author.

Title: The storyteller's sampler quilt : stitch 359 blocks to tell
your tale / Cinzia White.

Description: Lafayette, CA : C&T Publishing, Inc., [2019]

Identifiers: LCCN 2018050763 | ISBN 9781617458354 (soft cover)

Subjects: LCSH: Patchwork quilts. | Patchwork--Patterns. |
Storytelling in art.

Classification: LCC TT835 .W4935 2019 | DDC 746.46--dc23

LC record available at https://lccn.loc.gov/2018050763

Printed in China

10 9 8 7 6 5 4 3 2 1

Dedication

This book is dedicated to Paul, my husband, who has always given his encouragement through all of my endeavors. Without his support, my quilt *Raconteur—The Storyteller's Collection* would never have been finished and this book never started. To Paul-James and Richard, who, when young, helped to find lost pins and needles with their feet and now help to find lost files or fix frustrating software and computer problems. I love you always.

Acknowledgments

Many thanks go to all who contributed to the making of *The Storyteller's Sampler Quilt*. Special thanks go to Tim Manibusan and Linda Johnson for their patience and directions as I mastered the skills needed for presenting the diagrams; Roxane Cerda, Helen Frost, and Liz Aneloski, who encouraged and directed me throughout the entire process; and Alice Mace Nakanishi and the whole team at C&T for bringing my dream to fruition.

Contents

Collections

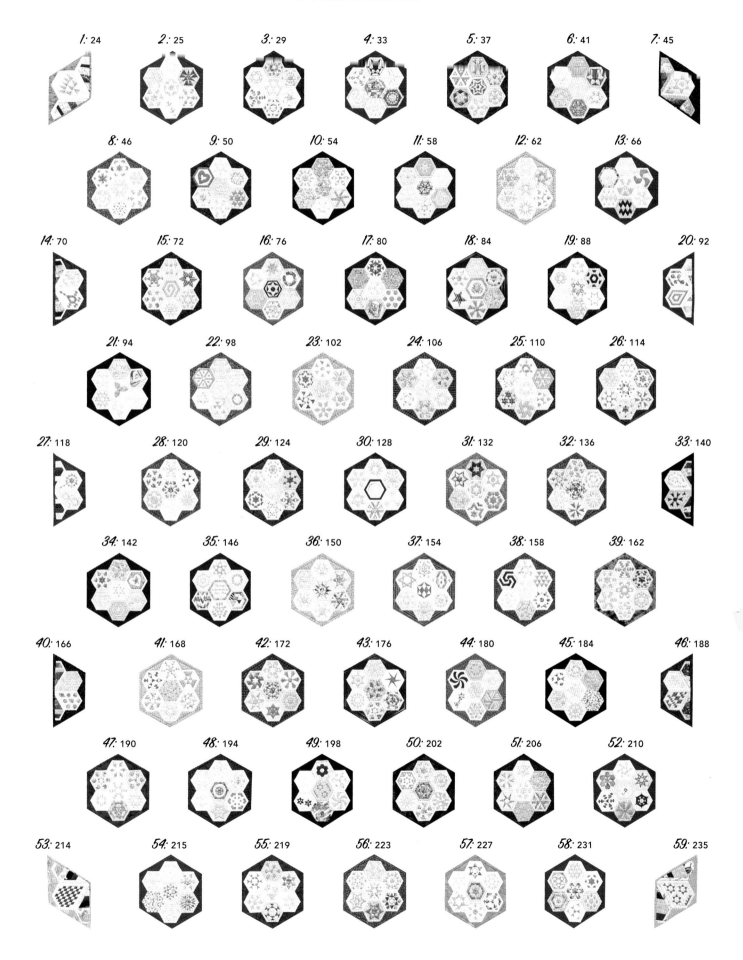

1: 24   2: 25   3: 29   4: 33   5: 37   6: 41   7: 45

8: 46   9: 50   10: 54   11: 58   12: 62   13: 66

14: 70   15: 72   16: 76   17: 80   18: 84   19: 88   20: 92

21: 94   22: 98   23: 102   24: 106   25: 110   26: 114

27: 118   28: 120   29: 124   30: 128   31: 132   32: 136   33: 140

34: 142   35: 146   36: 150   37: 154   38: 158   39: 162

40: 166   41: 168   42: 172   43: 176   44: 180   45: 184   46: 188

47: 190   48: 194   49: 198   50: 202   51: 206   52: 210

53: 214   54: 215   55: 219   56: 223   57: 227   58: 231   59: 235

Introduction

Having quilted for almost 30 years, I have reached a stage where I need to make quilts more than I need quilts, and it is to fulfill this need that I ventured into miniature quilt blocks. The *Raconteur—The Storyteller's Collection* quilt was designed as a take-anywhere project that I hoped would take me a while to finish. A block can take anywhere from one hour to one day to complete—but it is always fun.

The quilt title, *Raconteur—The Storyteller's Collection*, came about while I was working on designing new hexagonal blocks. When it came to naming the blocks, I started seeing in them significant people, places, and events that had shaped my life during the many years of the project. As I pieced the blocks and collections, the quilt became a story of my life and the people in it. An explanation of the names may be found on my website (page 247).

People's reactions to the finished blocks are delightful. *Raconteur* was planned so that when it was first seen from a distance, the viewer would see the Grandmother's Flower Garden arrangement, obvious through the dark-colored outer frames, with something glittering inside each one. As they approached, more details appeared until, standing directly before it, they could see the tiny individual pieces. Through the use of a subtle contrasting color of quilting thread, even the view from the back changes and reveals more as one approaches.

There is still no consensus on how many pieces are in the quilt. I calculated 13,937 while my husband, Paul, counted 14,084, and neither of us is willing to recount. The quickest block has just six pieces while the slowest to make has 147 pieces … all within a 2¼˝ hexagon.

Although I hand pieced more than 300 blocks, some of these are presented here as foundation piecing to speed up the process. Choose the method you prefer and have fun.

USING THIS BOOK

- **General Information** (page 7) contains information about overall construction of the quilt, including fabric quantities and types, preparing templates from patterns, and other techniques.

- **Completing the Collections** (page 15) offers guidance about the different types of collections, adding borders, and adding fillers; it also contains patterns for those pieces.

- **Collections** (page 24), which makes up the bulk of the book, contains instructions, illustrations, and full-size patterns for every block in the quilt's collections.

- **Completing the Quilt** (page 236) provides quilting instructions and some quilting designs.

- The **Gallery** (page 245) shows some other ways to use the blocks in this book.

General Information

Finished quilt: 95″ × 112″ • **Finished block:** Edge length 2¼″ • **Finished collection:** Edge length 7⅛″

Use the quilt photo (below) and quilt layout diagram (page 236) to match each collection with its number. The instructions and patterns for each collection's blocks are in Collections (page 24).

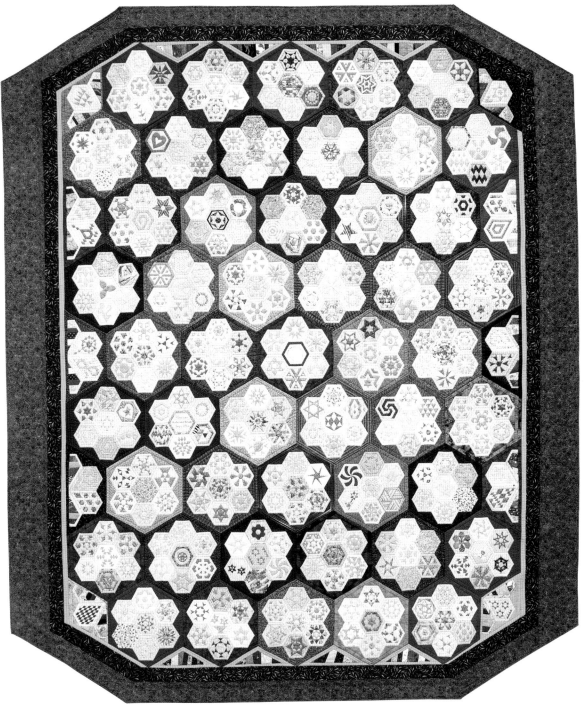

Raconteur—The Storyteller's Collection by Cinzia White

TERMINOLOGY

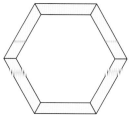

Block with mitered border

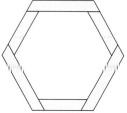

Block with long-short borders

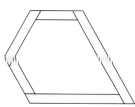

Extended hexagon with border

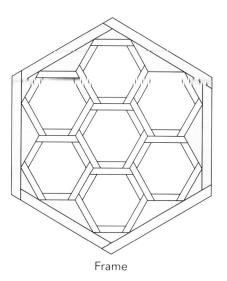

Frame

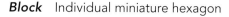

Block   Individual miniature hexagon

Border   Small strips surrounding each block, made from the same light fabric as the block

Full collection   Set of 7 blocks joined together and framed to make a complete unit

Side collection   Set of 4 blocks joined together and framed to make a complete unit

Corner collection   Set of 3 blocks joined together and framed to make a complete unit

Frame   Triangles and strips surrounding each collection

QAYG (quilt-as-you-go)   Process in which each framed collection is quilted before being joined to the neighboring collections or borders

SUPPLIES AND TOOLS

Freezer paper (such as Quilter's Freezer Paper Sheets by C&T Publishing)

Template plastic (such as Visi-GRID Quilter's Template Sheets by C&T Publishing)

Foundation paper (such as Carol Doak's Foundation Paper by C&T Publishing)

Lightweight fusible stabilizer

Lightweight paper for quilting designs (such as Golden Threads Quilting Paper)

Fabric scissors

Craft scissors

Ruler

Rotary cutting tools

Add-A-Quarter and Add-An-Eighth rulers (by CM Designs)

Fine-tip permanent markers (such as Pigma for fabric and Sharpie for template plastic)

Mechanical pencil

Sandpaper

Small resealable plastic bags

Iron and ironing board

Storing in Resealable Plastic Bags

Small resealable plastic bags are perfect for storage, especially because you may want to cut a number of blocks in one sitting after making the first one or two blocks.

FABRICS

- Choose 100% cotton, as it handles well and is easy to finger press.

- Large-scale prints are seldom suitable due to the miniature size of the blocks.

- To minimize color run, prewash and press your fabric.

- Requirements are based on 40″-wide fabric. The ¼″ seam allowance used throughout is included in the cutting measurements.

- Fabric quantities are approximate only; it is hard to describe or count the total number of prints chosen for this quilt. It is important that there is a contrast between the fabrics used in each block. Individual fabric amounts are *not* given for each block. Please note that …

  … a 10″ × 10″ square of light-value fabric is sufficient for 1 block and border.

  … 1 fat quarter of contrast fabric is sufficient for the dark of 3 blocks.

  … 1 fat quarter of a dark-value fabric is sufficient for 3 collection frames.

- The quilt is finished using quilt-as-you-go, and this uses significantly more fabric than normal.

Fabric Quantities

Light- to light medium-value fabrics: 90 fat quarters for backgrounds and borders of blocks

Medium- to dark medium-value fabrics: 60 fat quarters for contrast of blocks

Dark-value fabrics: 20 fat quarters for collection frames

Yellow stripe fabric: ⅔ yard for inner border, triangle filler borders, and corner collection borders

Purple print: 1¼ yards for middle border

Green tone-on-tone: 2¾ yards for outer border and binding

Backing: 11½ yards total for QAYG method

Batting: 6 yards for QAYG method

PREPARING TEMPLATES

Prepare templates from the patterns (pages 20–235), using one of the two following methods.

Using Freezer-Paper Templates

- *All templates are finished size except where marked.*
- *The seam allowance needs to be added when cutting fabric.*
- *The templates do not need to be reversed.*

I recommend using freezer-paper templates; once ironed to the fabric, they prevent slipping of the small pieces.

1. Using a ruler and mechanical pencil, trace the entire block pattern onto the dull side of freezer paper.

Trace around the patterns.

2. On each piece, write "dark" or "light," as appropriate.

3. Carefully cut along the lines to make the freezer-paper templates. Separate into dark and light piles.

4. With a dry iron, press the template pieces to the wrong side of the fabrics, leaving ½″ between the pieces for the seam allowance. Place the border and frame pieces parallel with the selvage where possible.

5. Using a mechanical pencil, trace around the freezer-paper template onto the fabric.

Prevent Stretching with Sandpaper

To prevent stretching the fabric, you can use a sandpaper board base while tracing.

6. Add a ¼″ seam allowance to all sides and cut the fabrics.

7. Place in a labeled resealable plastic bag.

Using Plastic Templates

- *All templates are finished size.*
- *The templates do not need to be reversed.*

Use templates made with template plastic where it is necessary to see the previous seamlines.

1. Using a ruler and fine-tip permanent marker, trace the pattern onto template plastic.

2. Write the template name on top.

3. Using craft scissors, cut on the marked lines.

4. Place the template on the wrong side of the fabric and mark the outer edge with a mechanical pencil. This is the sewing line.

5. Add a ¼″ seam allowance on all sides when cutting the fabrics.

PRESSING

Pressing seams toward the dark fabric is not always possible. Press abutting seams in opposing directions and fan intersections, if possible. When pressing, take care to not distort the block. I prefer to press hand-pieced blocks when complete and foundation-pieced blocks as I go.

REMOVING EXCESS SEAM ALLOWANCE

Due to the large amount of fabric in the seam allowances, the quilt may be quite heavy when finished. I suggest that you trim the seam allowances to ⅛″.

Doing this after a collection is completed, rather than as a block is completed, minimizes fraying on hand-pieced blocks. Foundation-pieced blocks should be trimmed as each seam is sewn. Don't be tempted to leave the excess seam allowance—it makes a difference.

TECHNIQUES

More than 300 blocks were hand pieced in *Raconteur*. This is my favorite method for many reasons, including portability, inclusiveness, and precision. Once the fabric is cut, the project can be completed anywhere—in front of the TV, while traveling, or when out with friends. It is perfect for social circles allowing conversations to flow.

Hand piecing is very forgiving and matching seams and perfect points are easily attained. Complicated blocks with tricky seams and many pieces may be finished accurately with hand piecing.

Prepare templates from patterns (pages 24–235) as needed.

Hand Piecing

1. Prepare freezer-paper templates and cut the fabrics (see Using Freezer-Paper Templates, page 9).

2. Using matching thread, join the pieces as shown.

3. Referring to Adding Borders (page 15), complete the block.

Hand Sewing

- Because the seams are short, use a fine needle to create a flat seam without holes. Sharps in sizes 9 or 10 are recommended.

- I always pin at the beginning and end of each seam and sometimes in the middle. I prefer to use appliqué pins, as these are short and less likely to catch the thread. The heads also make them easy to grasp.

- To sew the seams, always stitch along the drawn lines, using a short running stitch. Be sure not to sew across the seam allowances.

- To assist with accuracy, especially on curved seams, turn the pinned pieces over as you sew, checking that the needle remains on the line on both the front and the back.

- Piece with a thread color that matches the darker of two fabrics.

- Be sure *not* to knot at the beginning nor the end of a stitching line. Knots are too bulky for miniature quilts and may create a weak point.

- Begin and end each stitching line with a backstitch taken ¼″ from the corner, sew to the corner, and then reverse the sewing direction.

- When hand piecing border seams and frame seams, backstitch every 8–10 stitches to strengthen seams and control bias stretch.

Foundation Piecing

Preparing Pieces for Foundation Piecing

1. Copy foundation patterns onto lightweight paper. Be sure not to use muslin or interfacing as they are too bulky.

2. Referring to Using Freezer-Paper Templates (page 9), trace each separate pattern of the block once, leaving ¾˝ between the pieces.

3. Add a ⅜˝ seam allowance to all sides.

Add seam allowance.

4. Trim sharp triangle points to only ⅜˝ beyond the point. Place a ruler parallel to the bottom of the triangle and measure ⅜˝ beyond the point. Trim.

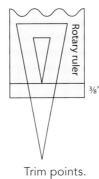

Trim points.

5. Write the cutting information on the template, and cut along the outer line.

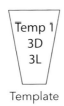

Template

6. Cut a strip of each fabric the width of tallest pattern piece. From the strip, cut the pieces as required. The seam allowance is included.

How to Foundation Piece

1. On the foundation paper, extend all seamlines ¼˝.

Extend seamlines.

2. Place the Piece 1 fabric on the back (blank side) of the foundation paper, with the wrong side of the fabric against the foundation paper.

3. Hold the paper up to a light source (with the printed design side of the paper facing you) to check that the piece of fabric is covering Foundation Piece 1 with at least a ¼˝ seam allowance on all sides. Pin or glue in place.

4. With right sides facing and with the edges aligned, place the Piece 2 fabric on the Piece 1 fabric. Pin to secure. Fold Fabric 2 back to check that it covers Piece 2.

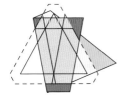

Align fabric edges.

5. Sew on the line on the foundation paper between Piece 1 and Piece 2, starting and finishing approximately ¼˝ beyond the seamline. For best results, use a fine machine needle and sew with 12–14 stitches to the inch.

6. Finger press the seam flat. Check that Fabric 2 completely covers Piece 2, with at least a ¼˝ seam allowance on all sides. If it does not, remove the stitches and resew. Press again with an iron.

7. Fold the fabric and paper back, exposing the sewn seam. Use a bookmark or card on the seam for a crisp edge. Trim *only* the seam allowance back to ⅛˝ using the Add-An-Eighth ruler. Be sure *not* to cut the foundation paper.

8. Place a bookmark along the next seam.

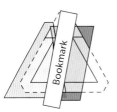

Place bookmark.

9. Fold the foundation paper back over the bookmark and trim excess Fabric 1 to ¼″.

Fold foundation paper back.

10. Align Fabric 3 to the Fabric 1 edge.

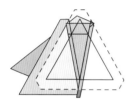

Align fabric edges.

11. Pin to secure, turn over, and stitch on the marked line as before.

12. Continue in the same manner, repeating Steps 6–11 until you have sewn all pieces to the paper.

13. When complete, trim each side ¼″ out from the solid outer line.

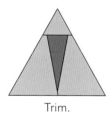

Trim.

14. Carefully remove the papers, taking care not to disturb the stitches. *Note:* Tweezers may be helpful in removing paper from tight areas.

15. Sew together the sections as shown in the diagrams.

16. Referring to Adding Borders (page 15), complete the block.

Appliqué

You may complete appliqué blocks using your preferred method, with hand or machine sewing. Most of the appliqué blocks I made for this quilt were made using the needle-turn method.

1. Prepare Template B (page 20) using template plastic (see Using Plastic Templates, page 10).

2. Trace the appliqué templates on the right side of the fabric, leaving a generous ½″ between shapes.

3. Cut out each shape ¼″ outside the traced lines.

4. Pin or glue each shape in place on a 6″ × 6″ fabric square, referring to the design for placement.

5. Needle-turn appliqué all the shapes with cotton threads to match the fabrics, using the tip and side of the needle to roll the edge of the fabric under the drawn line, and blindstitch in place.

6. Clip or notch the curves where needed to help the shapes lie flat on the background fabric.

7. On the back of the block, center Template B on the design and trace using a mechanical pencil.

8. Add a ¼″ seam allowance and trim the fabric.

9. Referring to Adding Borders (page 15), complete the block.

Embroidery

1. Prepare Template B (page 20) using template plastic (see Using Plastic Templates, page 10).

2. With a dry iron, press a 6″ × 6″ square of freezer paper to the back of a 6″ × 6″ square of fabric.

3. Using a lightbox and a fine-tip permanent pen, transfer the design to the front of the fabric. Be sure not to draw the block outline on the front.

4. Fuse a stabilizer to the back of the fabric.

5. Using a single thread of stranded cotton, use a back-stitch to stitch the design in the given colors.

6. Press from the back.

7. On the back of the block, center Template B on the design and trace using a mechanical pencil.

8. Add a ¼″ seam allowance and trim the fabric.

9. Referring to Adding Borders (page 15), complete the block.

Trimming Oversize Blocks

1. Prepare Template B in template plastic (see Using Plastic Templates, page 10).

2. On the wrong side of the block, center Template B on the design and trace using a mechanical pencil.

3. Add the seam allowance and trim the fabric.

4. Referring to Adding Borders (page 15), complete the block.

Partial Seams

In some instances, it is necessary to first sew only part of a seam. The seam is completed after other parts of the block have been added.

1. Looking closely at the block, note the seams that don't meet end to end.

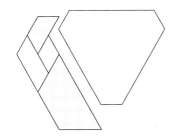

2. Align the sides and begin sewing at the end where the pieces meet. Sew until you reach approximately ½″ from the end.

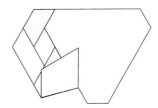

3. Backstitch and cut the thread.

4. Align the sides with the next piece, and sew end to end.

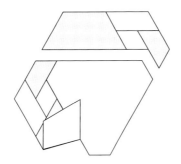

5. Work around the block until you return to the original seam. Complete this seam last.

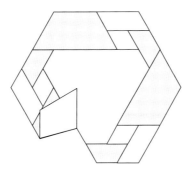

English Paper Piecing

I did not use the English paper piecing method for making any of the blocks, however, Carol LeMaitre completed many blocks this way (see Gallery, page 246). Due to the large number of pieces in such a small block and the resulting large number of seams, it was necessary to scale some blocks. Carol used a ScanNCut (by Brother International Corp.) to cut her papers from card stock (such as manila file folders / 200 gsm paper). Although it was necessary to further scale some of the blocks, our rule was to scale blocks with more than 48 pieces by 98%.

If using English paper piecing, sew the block, remove the papers in the outer edge, and press the edge seam allowance outward. Using a plastic Template B (page 20), mark the block edge on the back of the fabric, and add the long-short borders by machine.

Danni Reynolds (see Gallery, page 246) used Eppiflex English Paper Piecing Templates (available from The Quilting Patch, e-patch.com.au) to make an enlarged version. Using the larger size blocks, she found no extra scaling was needed to compensate for the difference in the number of pieces.

CENTER STARS

Stars are central to many blocks. They are usually constructed in one of three ways, depending on the final appearance.

Basic Star

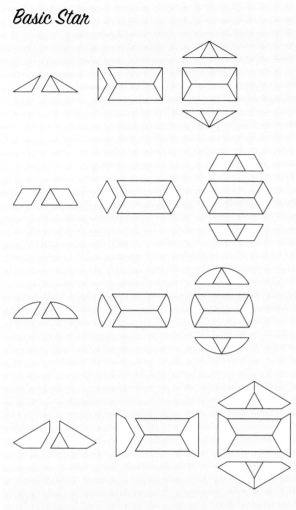

For each:

1. Make 2 of the top and bottom sections.

2. Make 1 of the center section.

3. Join.

Star with a Central Hexagon

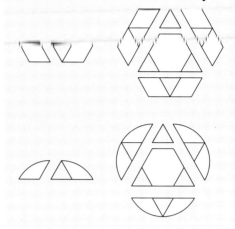

For each:

1. Make 3 of the outer sections.

2. Make 1 of the center section.

3. Join.

Star in a Triangle

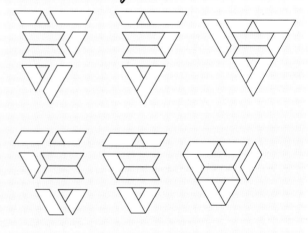

For each:

1. Make 1 of each section.

2. Join.

Completing the Collections

Prepare templates from the patterns (page 20) as directed in the instructions below.

ADDING BORDERS

Due to the small size and often large number of pieces, it may be difficult making the final block size accurate, so I have added an additional fudge factor into the block border templates. The "accurate" border width is marked with a dashed line in Templates C–E. The solid line, beyond the dashed line, allows the finished block to be trimmed to the correct size. Instructions are written assuming the templates have been made using the solid line.

Mitered Borders

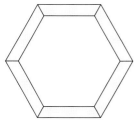

Block with mitered borders

The blocks in *Raconteur* have mitered borders. This gives a formal frame to the blocks; however, it results in crowded intersections where 3 blocks meet.

1. Prepare Template A (page 20), using template plastic (see Using Plastic Templates, page 10).

2. Prepare Template C (page 20), using freezer paper and the same background fabric as the block (see Using Freezer-Paper Templates, page 9).

3. Sew the Template C pieces to the block.

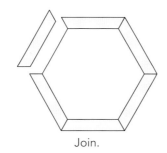

Join.

4. On the back of the block, center Template A and use a fine mechanical pencil to mark the outer edge. This is the next sewing line. Ignore all the other previously drawn lines. The design area should lie within the dashed lines.

5. Add a ¼˝ seam allowance and trim the fabric.

Short-Long Borders

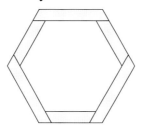

Block with short-long borders

Using short-long borders is an easier border option.

1. Prepare Template A (page 20), using template plastic (see Using Plastic Templates, page 10).

2. Prepare Templates D (page 20) and E (page 20), using freezer paper and the same background fabric as the block (see Using Freezer-Paper Templates, page 9).

3. Sew the Template D pieces then the Template E pieces to the block.

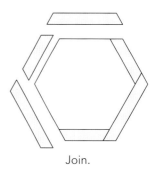

Join.

4. Refer to Mitered Borders, Steps 4 and 5 (at left), to finish.

Extended Hexagon Borders

MATERIALS

• 1¼˝ × 25˝ strip of same fabric as block background

CONSTRUCTION

1. Prepare Template F (page 20), using template plastic (see Using Plastic Templates, page 10).

2. Trim the completed extended hexagon block ¼″ beyond the outer solid line.

3. Sew strips to the short sides. Press and trim them even with the edges.

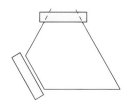

4. Sew strips to the other sides. Press and trim them even with the edges.

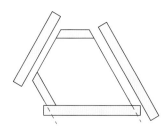

5. On the back, matching the seams to the dashed lines, place Template F on the block.

6. Using a mechanical pencil, mark the finished block size. This line is the next sewing line.

7. Add a ¼″ seam allowance and trim the fabric.

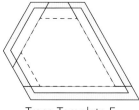

Trace Template F.

COMPLETING A FULL COLLECTION

MATERIALS

7 blocks

• 6″ × 18″ dark-value fabric for frames

CONSTRUCTION

1. Ensure all blocks are the same size. Check the sizes, using Template A (page 20), and adjust if needed.

2. Prepare Templates G, H, J, and K (pages 20 and 21), using freezer-paper templates (see Using Freezer-Paper Templates, page 9).

3. From the dark-value fabric, cut 6 Templates G–H and 3 Templates J–K, adding the seam allowance to all pieces.

4. Join 7 blocks, and press.

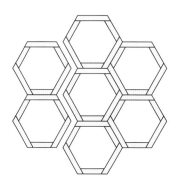

5. Sew Templates G and H to the collection, and press.

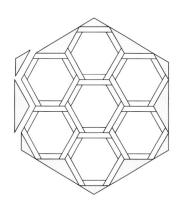

6. Sew Templates J and K to the collection, and press.

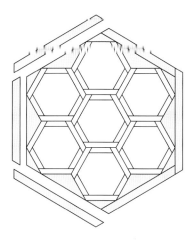

7. Trim the excess seam allowance to ⅛″ on all block seams.

COMPLETING A FULL COLLECTION WITH EXTENSION

Full collections that are placed on the sides of the quilt (positions 8, 13, 21, 26, 34, 39, 47 and 52; see Layout, page 236) need an extra frame added to the outer edge.

1. Complete the collection as detailed in Completing a Full Collection (at left).

2. Prepare Template L (page 21), using freezer-paper templates and the same fabric as the original frame (see Using Freezer-Paper Templates, page 9).

3. For Collections 8, 21, 34, and 47, sew Template L to the right-hand edge, and press.

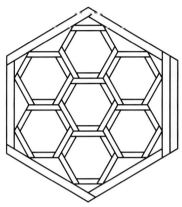

Collections 8, 21, 34, and 47

4. For Collections 13, 26, 39, and 52, sew Template L to the left-hand edge, and press.

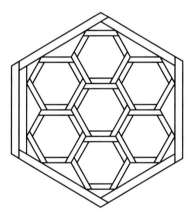

Collections 13, 26, 39, and 52

FILLER BLOCKS

Filler blocks are needed in the side and corner collections and also along the top and bottom of the quilt to straighten the edges. Within these collections, the split extended hexagons are mirror images of each other. All are made using a variety of scraps in all values.

Split Extended Hexagon Fillers

MATERIALS

• Variety of scraps ½″–3″ wide

• 1¼″ × 22″ strip of medium-value fabric for border

CONSTRUCTION

1. Prepare Template M (page 21), using freezer paper (see Using Freezer-Paper Templates, page 9).

2. Prepare Template N (page 21), using template plastic (see Using Plastic Templates, page 10).

3. Choose strips of fabric of different colors, prints, and widths. Shorten the stitch length to 2 and sew together the strips lengthwise.

4. Continue adding strips until the set is larger than Template M.

5. Press all the seams away from the point, and press Template M to the unit.

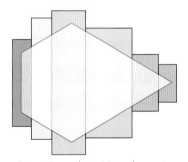

Press Template M to the unit.

6. Using rotary cutting equipment, carefully cut around the template. *Note:* The seam allowance is included in the template.

7. Add strips to the short sides, and trim even with the edges.

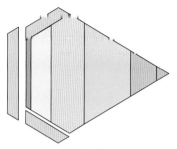

Add borders.

8. Cut the unit in half.

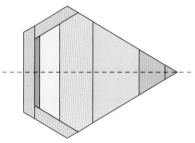

Cut in half.

9. Add a strip to the angled side, and trim it even with the edges.

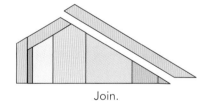

Join.

10. On the back, matching the border seams to the dashed lines, place Template L on the block. Using a mechanical pencil, trace around the template to mark the sewing lines. There is no border on the long straight side.

11. Add a ¼″ seam allowance to *all sides* and trim.

12. Make 10 sets of 2.

Triangle Fillers

MATERIALS

- Variety of scraps ½″–3″ wide
- 1¼″ × 34″ strip of yellow fabric for border

CONSTRUCTION

1. Prepare Template O (page 22), using freezer paper (see Using Freezer-Paper Templates, page 9).

2. Prepare Template P (page 23), using template plastic (see Using Plastic Templates, page 10).

3. Choose strips of fabric of different colors, prints, and widths. Shorten the stitch length to 2, and sew together the strips lengthwise.

4. Continue adding strips until the set is larger than Template O.

5. Press all the seams away from the point, and press Template O to the unit.

6. Using rotary cutting equipment, carefully cut around the template. *Note:* The seam allowance is included in the template.

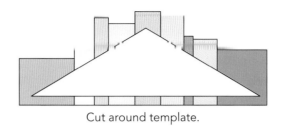

Cut around template.

7. Sew border strips (see Split Extended Hexagon Fillers, page 17) to all sides.

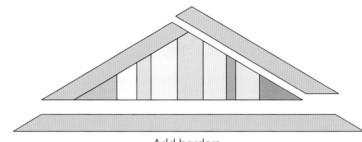

Add borders.

8. On the wrong side of the fabric, matching the border seams to the dashed lines, place Template P on the block. Using a mechanical pencil, trace around the template to mark the sewing lines.

9. Add a ¼″ seam allowance to all sides and trim.

10. Make 8.

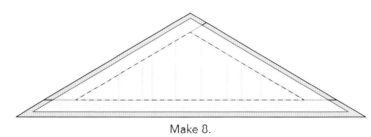

Make 8.

COMPLETING A SIDE COLLECTION

MATERIALS

- 2 extended hexagons
- 2 extended hexagon fillers
- 6″ × 18″ strip of dark-value fabric for frames

CONSTRUCTION

Some templates need to be the mirror image of others. The reversed patterns for these templates are labeled with the template letter and the abbreviation "(rev)."

1. Prepare Templates G–I and I (rev) (page 20) and Templates Q–S and R (rev) (page 22), using freezer paper (see Using Freezer-Paper Templates, page 9).

2. Cut 2 of Template G, 3 of Template H, and 1 each of

Templates I, I (rev), Q–S, and R (rev), adding a ¼″ seam allowance to all pieces.

3. Arrange the blocks and fillers. Matching the end points, sew together. Press.

4. Add the frame triangles and the short frame (Template Q). Press the seam allowance outward.

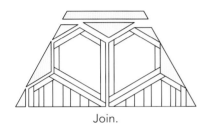

Join.

5. Add the remaining frames (Templates R and S). Press the seam allowance outward.

Join.

6. Complete the side collection.

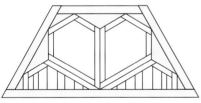

Completed side collection

COMPLETING A CORNER COLLECTION

MATERIALS

- 1 extended hexagon
- 2 extended hexagon fillers
- 6″ × 10″ strip of dark-value fabric for frames

CONSTRUCTION

1. Prepare Templates G–I and I (rev) (page 20) and Templates T, U, and U (rev) (page 23), using the freezer paper (see Using Freezer-Paper Templates, page 9).

2. From the frame fabric, cut 2 of Template H and 1 each of Templates G, I, I (rev), T, U, and U (rev), adding the seam allowance to all the pieces.

3. Arrange the blocks and the frame pieces as shown.

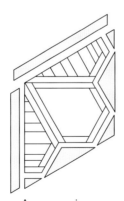

Arrange pieces.

4. Sew together. Press the seam allowance outward. Make 4.

5. Attach Template U (rev) to Collections 1 and 59. Make 2.

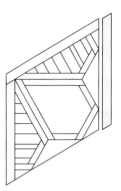

Collections 1 and 59

6. Attach Template T to Collections 7 and 53. Make 2.

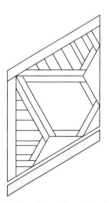

Collections 7 and 53

PATTERNS

When making templates from these patterns, add a ¼˝ seam allowance to all templates unless marked otherwise.

The individual block patterns can be found in Collections (page 24).

I

I (rev)

B

A

H

E

D

C

F

G

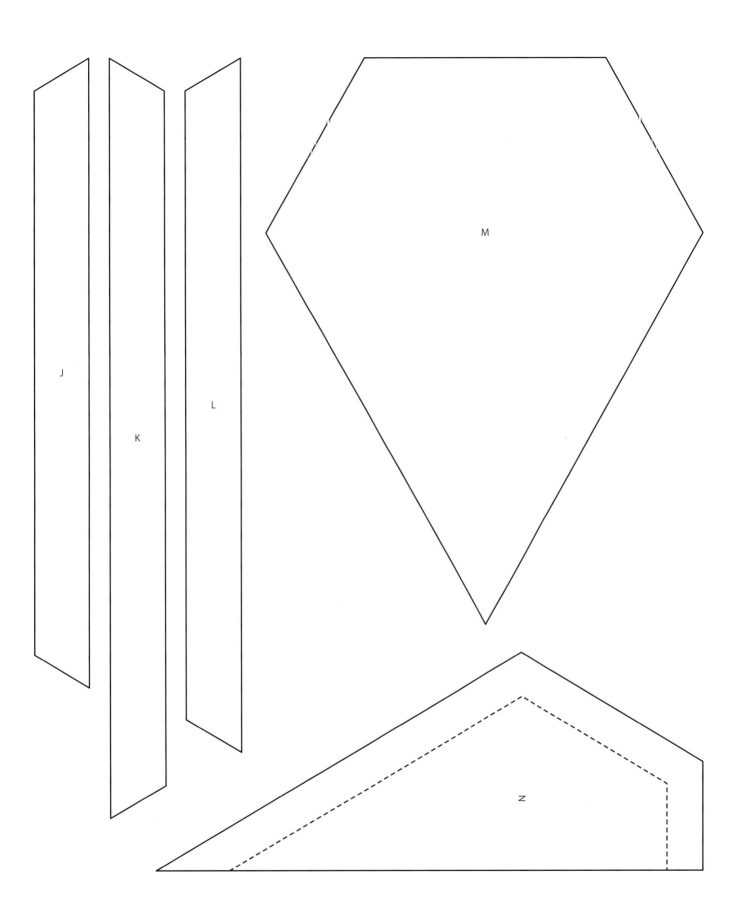

J

K

L

M

Z

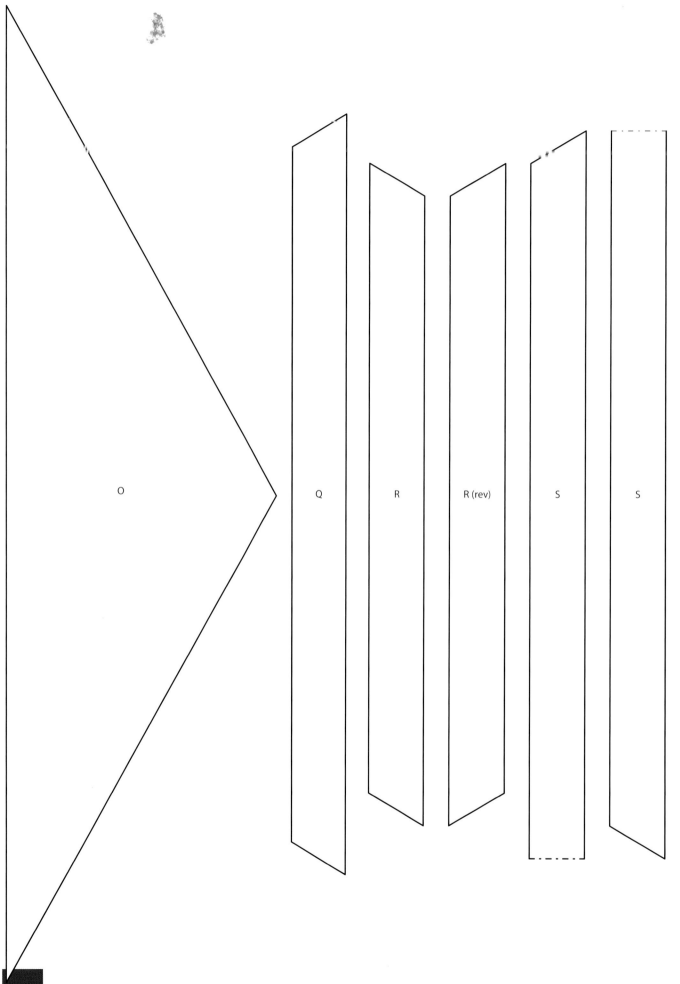

O

Q

R

R (rev)

S

S

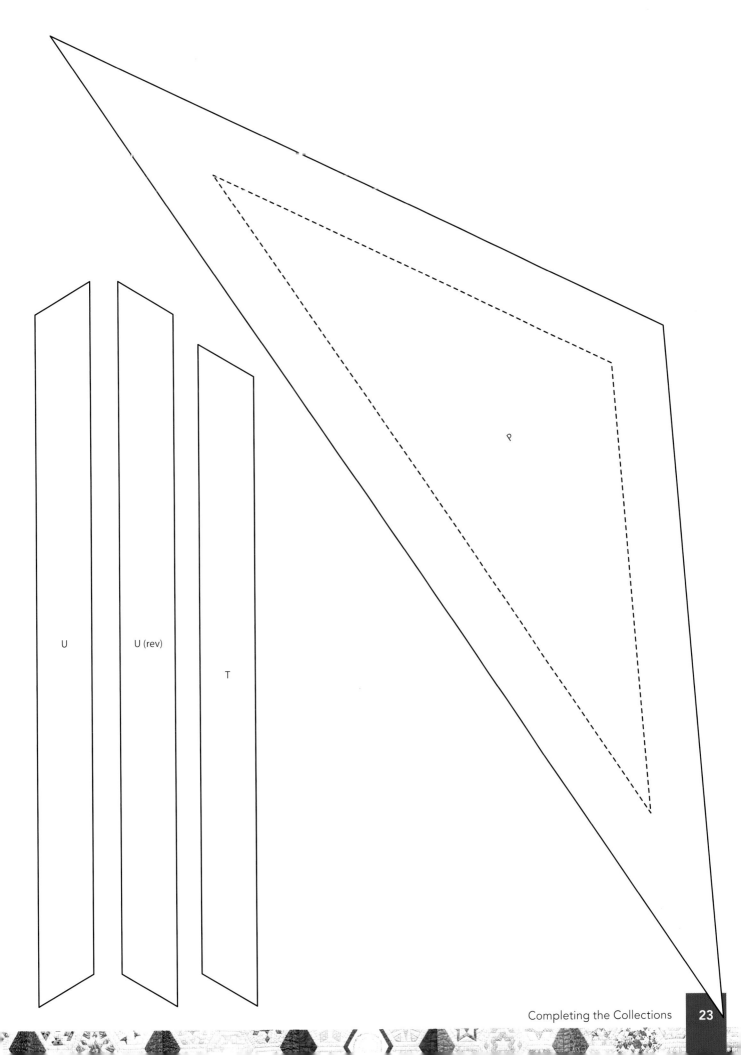

U

U (rev)

T

P

Collections

There are 59 collections with a total of 359 blocks. Each block lists the techniques to refer to while making it.

Refer to General Information (page 7) and Completing the Collections (page 15) as needed.

The patterns are shown in a neutral shade, suitable for tracing. The construction illustrations are shown in the colors of the blocks. Patterns for asymmetrical blocks are shown reversed, since the templates will be traced on the wrong side of the fabrics. All blocks may be rotated to match, or not match, the photos as desired.

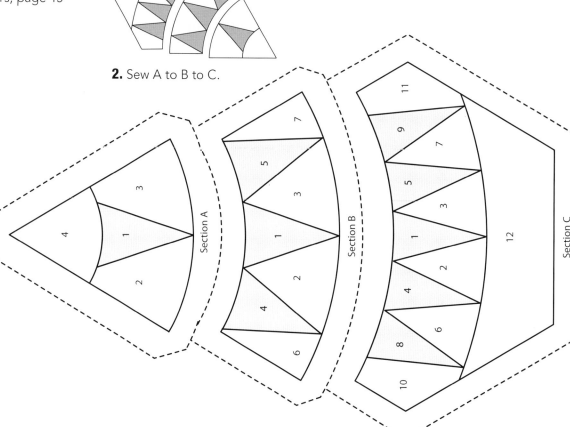

Crowning Grace

TECHNIQUES

Foundation piecing, page 11

Hand piecing, page 10

Adding borders, page 15

1. Make 1 of each.

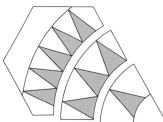

2. Sew A to B to C.

Section A

Section B

Section C

Café Crème

TECHNIQUES

Hand piecing, page 10

Center stars, page 14

Adding borders, page 15

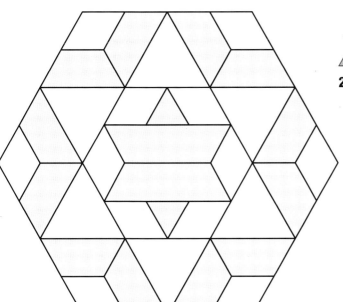

1. Make 1.

2. Make 6.

3. Join; make 3.

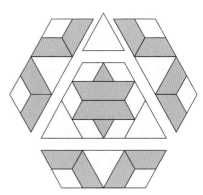

4. Join.

Crème de Chantilly

TECHNIQUES

Hand piecing, page 10

Adding borders, page 15

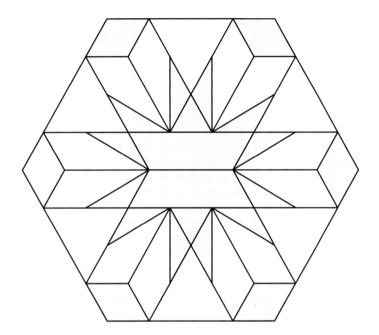

1. Make 4.

2. Make 2.

3. Make 2.

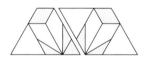

4. Join; make 2.

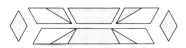

5. Join.

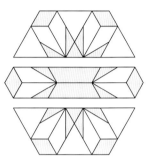

6. Join.

A Merry Xmas

TECHNIQUES

Foundation piecing, page 11

Adding borders, page 15

1. Make 3 of each.

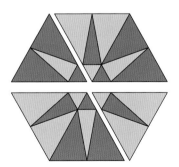

2. Join.

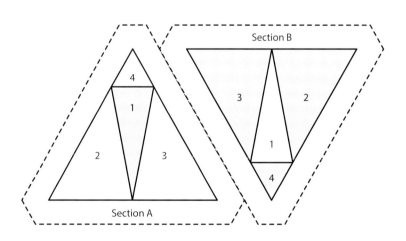

Flamboyance

TECHNIQUES

Hand piecing, page 10

Adding borders, page 15

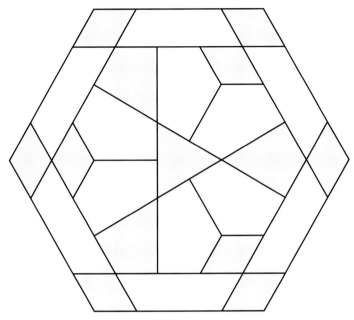

1. Make 3.

2. Make 2.

3. Join.

4. Make 3.

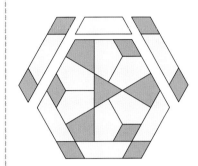

5. Join.

The Rice Pickers

TECHNIQUES

Hand piecing, page 10

Adding borders, page 15

1. Make 1.

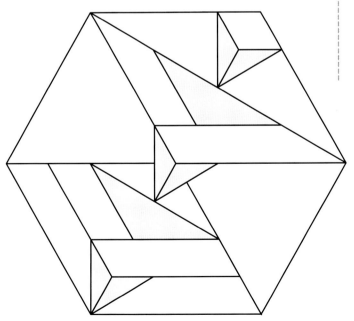

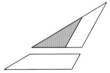

2. Make 1.

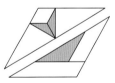

3. Join.

4. Make 1.

5. Make 1.

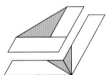

6. Join.

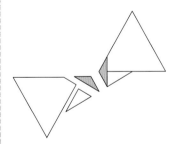

7. Make 1.

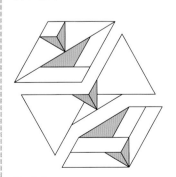

8. Join.

I Love Lucy

TECHNIQUES

Hand piecing, page 10

Partial seams, page 13

Center stars, page 14

Adding borders, page 15

1. Make 1.

2. Make 3.

3. Make 3.

4. Join; make 3.

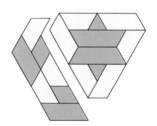

5. Join with a partial seam.

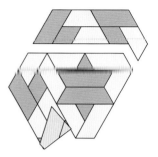

6. Join.

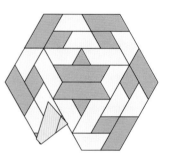

7. Join; complete the partial seam.

Not Here Thanks

TECHNIQUES

Foundation piecing, page 11

Adding borders, page 15

1. Make 1 of each.

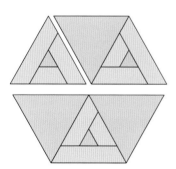

2. Join.

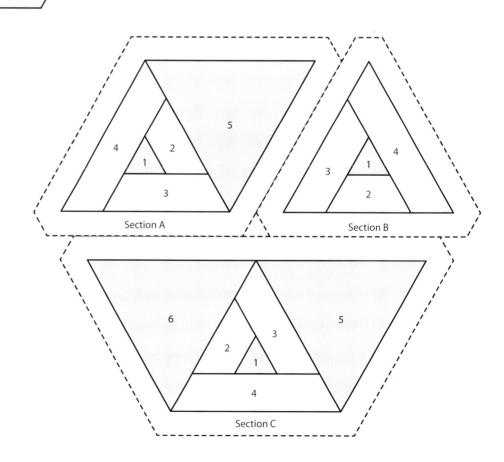

Section A

Section B

Section C

Fox Pawed

TECHNIQUES

Hand piecing, page 10

Adding borders, page 15

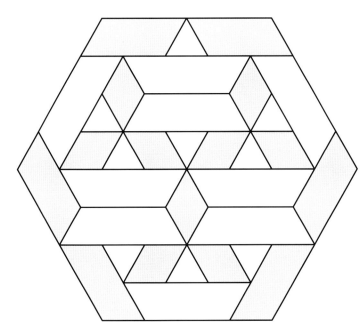

1. Make 1.

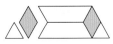

2. Make 1.

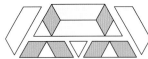

3. Join.

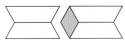

4. Make 1.

5. Join.

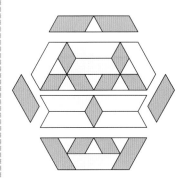

6. Join.

Ketchikan Jewels

TECHNIQUES

Hand piecing, page 10

Adding borders, page 15

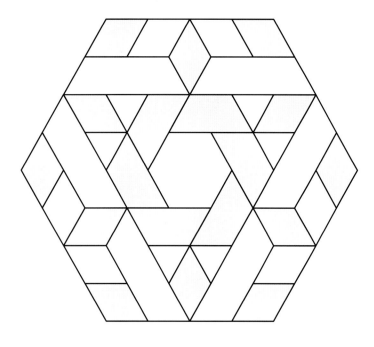

1. Make 3.

2. Make 3.

3. Join.

4. Join.

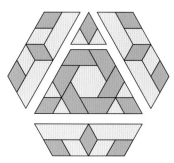

5. Join.

After the Showers

TECHNIQUES

Hand piecing, page 10

Adding borders, page 15

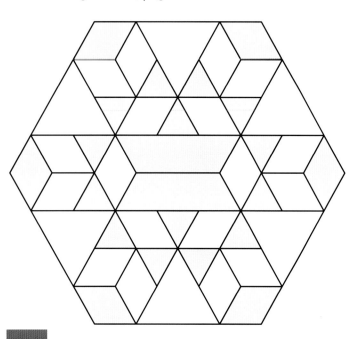

1. Make 6.

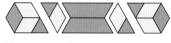

2. Join; make 1.

3. Make 4.

4. Make 2.

5. Make 2.

6. Join; make 2.

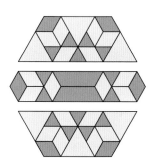

7. Join.

Burning Bright

TECHNIQUES

Hand piecing, page 10

Adding borders, page 15

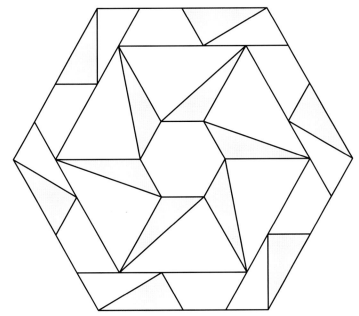

1. Make 6.

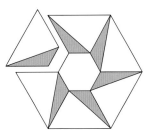

2. Join.

3. Make 6.

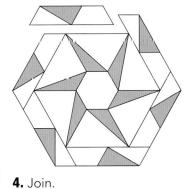

4. Join.

Raspberry Swirl

TECHNIQUES

Hand piecing, page 10

Center stars, page 14

Adding borders, page 15

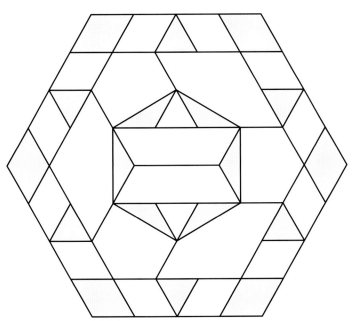

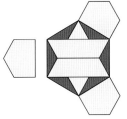

1. Make 1; join.

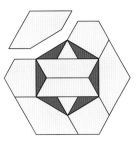

2. Join.

3. Make 3.

4. Make 3.

5. Join.

One to the Left

TECHNIQUES

Hand piecing, page 10

Adding borders, page 15

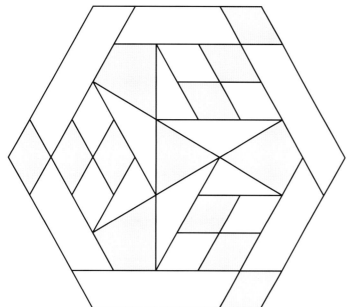

1. Make 3.

2. Make 3.

3. Make 2.

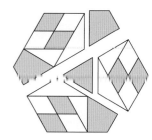

4. Join.

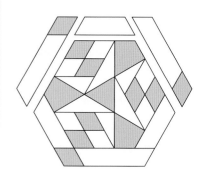

5. Join.

Paprika

TECHNIQUES

Hand piecing, page 10

Adding borders, page 15

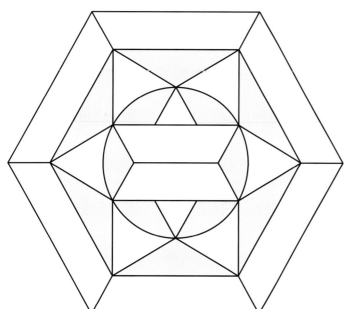

1. Make 6.

2. Join; make 1.

3. Make 6.

4. Join; make 2.

5. Join; make 2.

6. Join; make 2.

7. Join.

Green with Ivy

TECHNIQUES

Machine piecing

Trimming oversize blocks, page 13

Adding borders, page 15

Cut 4 strips ⅞˝ × 7½˝ of both colors; join.

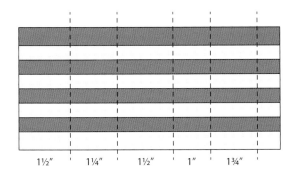

| 1½" | 1¼" | 1½" | 1" | 1¾" |

1. Cut 5 strips, as shown.

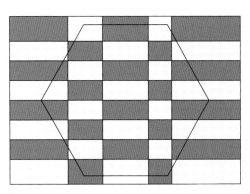

2. Rotate 2 strips; join and press.

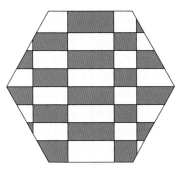

3. Trim.

Blackberry Freedom

TECHNIQUES

Hand piecing, page 10

Adding borders, page 15

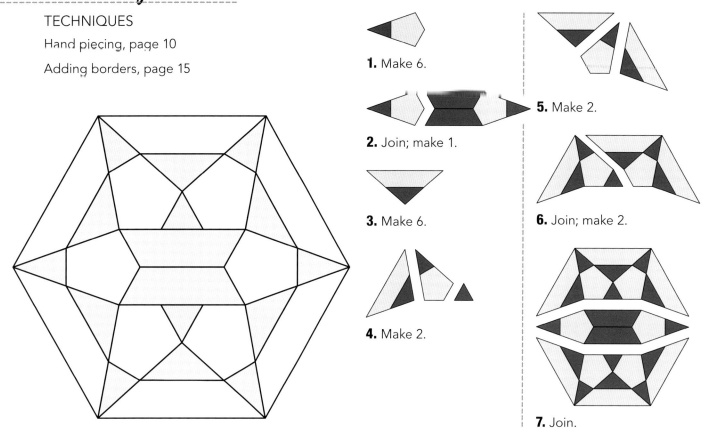

1. Make 6.

2. Join; make 1.

3. Make 6.

4. Make 2.

5. Make 2.

6. Join; make 2.

7. Join.

Rainbow Semaphore

TECHNIQUES

Foundation piecing, page 11

Adding borders, page 15

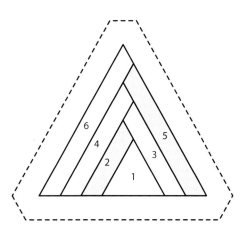

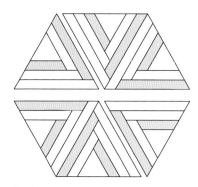

1. Make 6.

2. Join.

New Beginnings

TECHNIQUES

Foundation piecing, page 11

Appliqué, page 12

Trimming oversize blocks, page 13

Adding borders, page 15

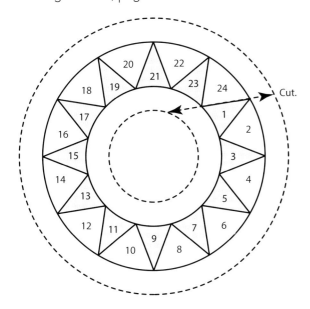

1. Cut along *all* the dotted lines.

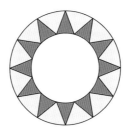

2. Make 1; join ends.

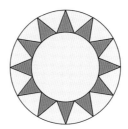

3. Appliqué the center circle.

4. Appliqué to the center of a 6″ × 6″ square.

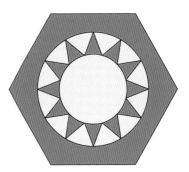

5. Trim.

Summer's Day

TECHNIQUES

Hand piecing, page 10

Adding borders, page 15

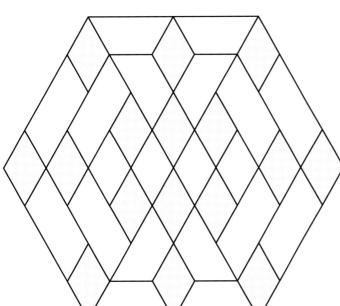

1. Make 2.

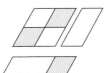

2. Join; make 2.

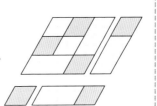

3. Join; make 2.

4. Make 2.

5. Join.

Your Decision

TECHNIQUES

Hand piecing, page 10

Adding borders, page 15

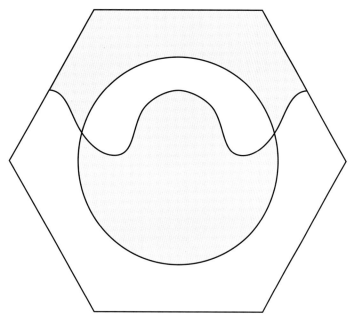

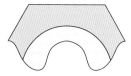

1. Make 1.

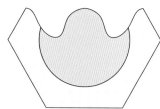

2. Make 1.

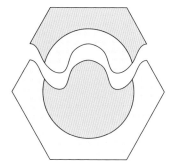

3. Join.

Birds at the Window

TECHNIQUES

Hand piecing, page 10

Adding borders, page 15

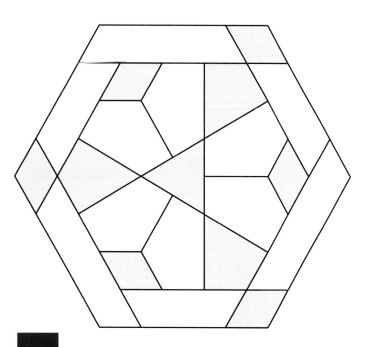

1. Make 3.

2. Make 2.

3. Make 1.

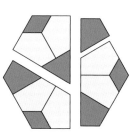

4. Join.

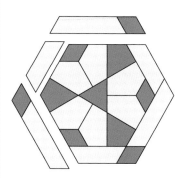

5. Join.

Echoes

TECHNIQUES

Hand piecing, page 10

Partial seams, page 13

Center stars, page 14

Adding borders, page 15

1. Make 3.

2. Join; make 1.

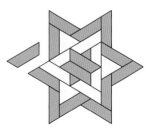

3. Join.

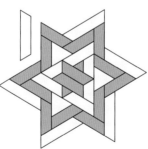

4. Join.

5. Join with partial seams.

Gift Wrapped

TECHNIQUES

Hand piecing, page 10

Adding borders, page 15

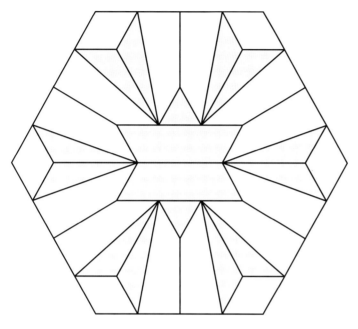

1. Make 6.

2. Make 6.

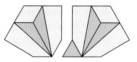

3. Join; make 2.

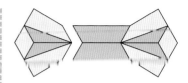

4. Join; make 1.

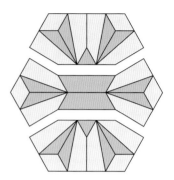

5. Join.

Pointing the Finger

TECHNIQUES

Hand piecing, page 10

Adding borders, page 15

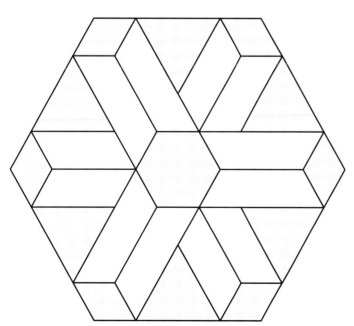

1. Make 3.

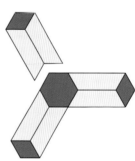

2. Join.

3. Make 3.

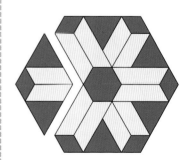

4. Join.

Baby Blue

TECHNIQUES

Hand piecing, page 10

Adding borders, page 15

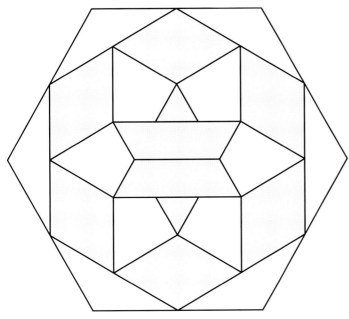

1. Make 2.

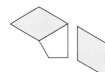

2. Make 2.

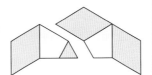

3. Join; make 2.

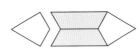

4. Join; make 1.

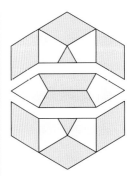

5. Join.

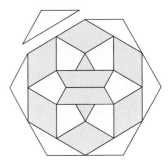

6. Join.

Taylor's World

TECHNIQUES

Hand piecing, page 10

Adding borders, page 15

1. Make 3.

2. Make 3.

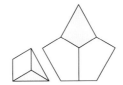

3. Make 2.

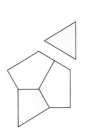

4. Make 1.

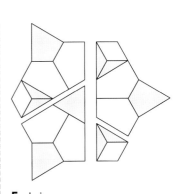

5. Join.

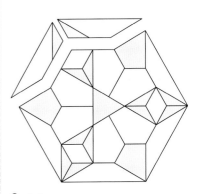

6. Join.

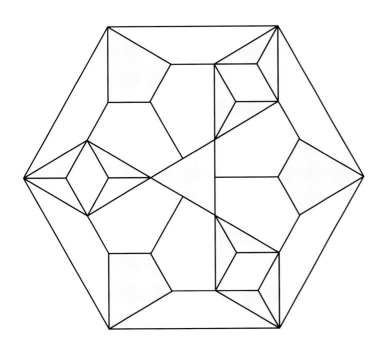

Collections **39**

Mums Among the Gold

TECHNIQUES

Hand piecing, page 10

Center stars, page 14

Adding borders, page 15

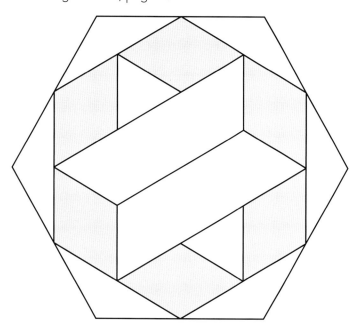

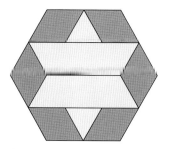

1. Make 1.

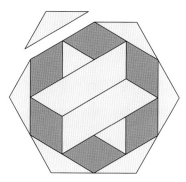

2. Join.

Behind the Walls

TECHNIQUES

Foundation piecing, page 11

Adding borders, page 15

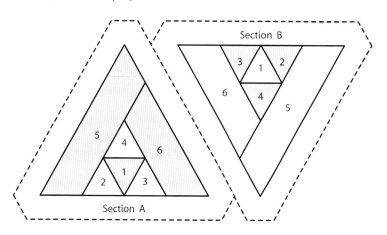

1. Make 3 of each.

2. Join.

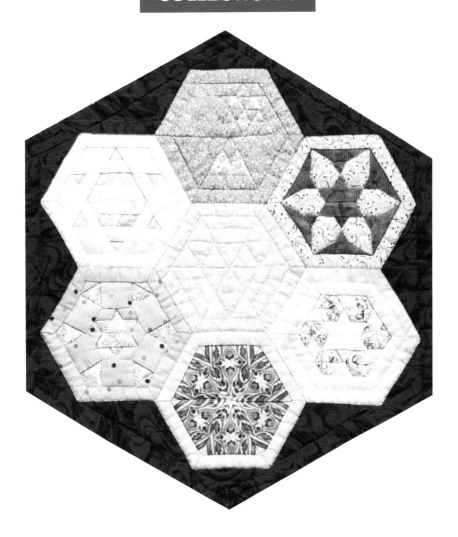

Enter with Care

TECHNIQUES

Foundation piecing, page 11

Adding borders, page 15

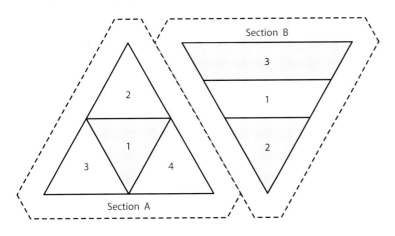

Section B

3

1

2

2

1

3 4

Section A

1. Make 3 of each.

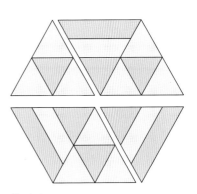

2. Join.

Crystal Dreams

TECHNIQUES

Hand piecing, page 10

Adding borders, page 15

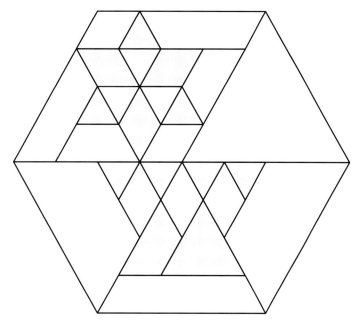

1. Make 1.

2. Make 1.

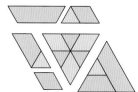

3. Make 1.

4. Make 1.

5. Make 2.

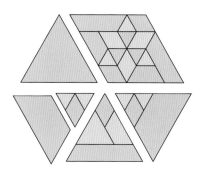

6. Join.

Disappearing Hope

TECHNIQUES

Hand piecing, page 10

Adding borders, page 15

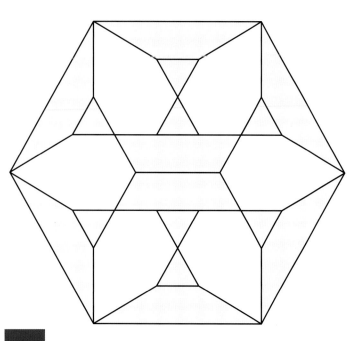

1. Make 4.

2. Make 2.

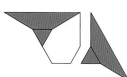

3. Make 2.

4. Join; make 2.

5. Join; make 1.

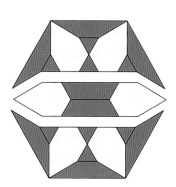

6. Join.

Short Changed

TECHNIQUES

Hand piecing, page 10

Partial seams, page 13

Adding borders, page 15

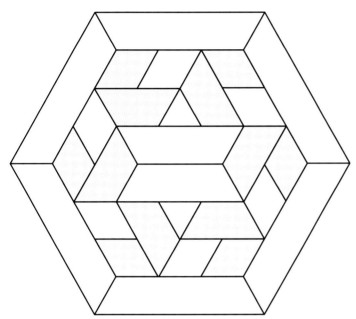

1. Make 6.

2. Make 2.

3. Make 2.

4. Join with partial seams.

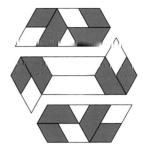

5. Join.

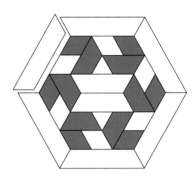

6. Join.

With Care

TECHNIQUES

Foundation piecing, page 11

Adding borders, page 15

The fabric is fussy cut.

1. Make 2.

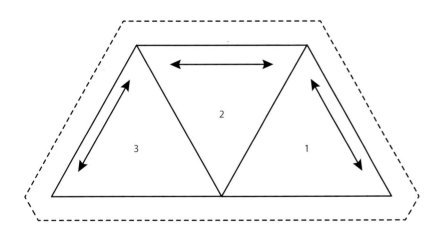

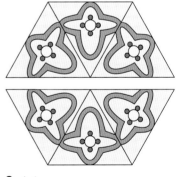

2. Join.

Fake Hands

TECHNIQUES

Hand piecing, page 10

Center stars, page 14

Adding borders, page 15

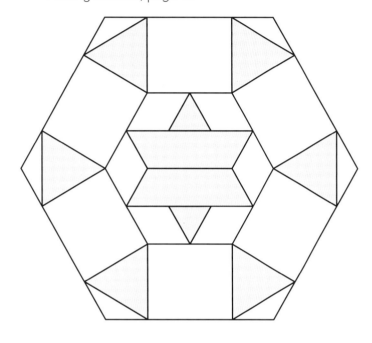

1. Make 1.

2. Make 6.

3. Make 2.

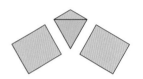

4. Make 2.

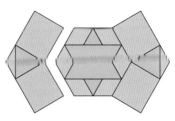

5. Join.

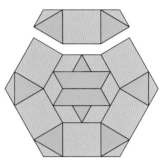

6. Join.

Strung Out

TECHNIQUES

Hand piecing, page 10

Center stars, page 14

Adding borders, page 15

1. Make 1.

2. Make 3.

3. Join.

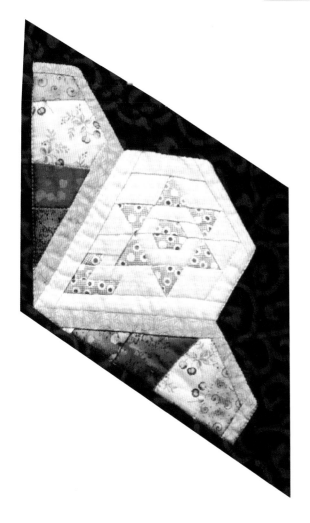

Merry Margaret

TECHNIQUES

Foundation piecing, page 11

Adding borders, page 15

1. Make 1 of each.

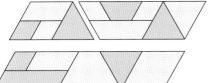

2. Sew CD to E.

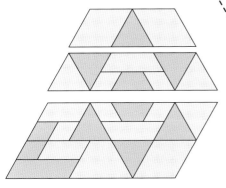

3. Join.

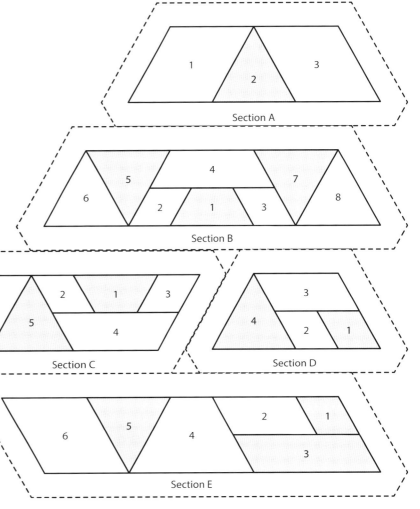

Section A

Section B

Section C

Section D

Section E

Too Many Thorns

TECHNIQUES

Hand piecing, page 10

Center stars, page 14

Adding borders, page 15

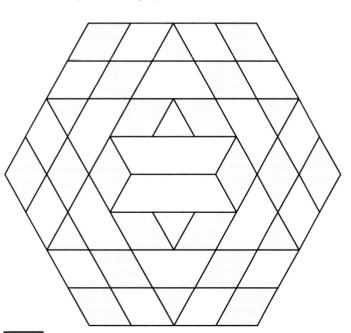

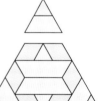

1. Make 1; join.

2. Make 6.

3. Join; make 3.

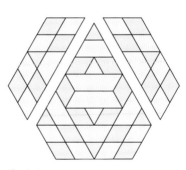

4. Join.

Banana Custard

TECHNIQUES

Hand piecing, page 10

Adding borders, page 15

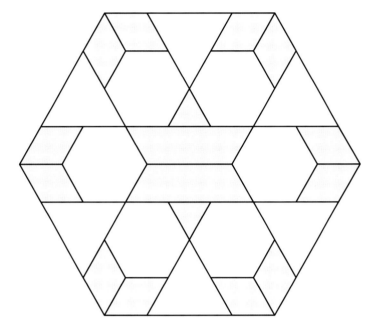

1. Make 6.

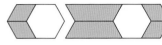

2. Join; make 1.

3. Make 4.

4. Make 2.

5. Make 2.

6. Join; make 2.

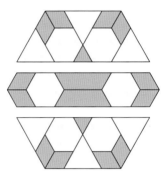

7. Join.

City Living

TECHNIQUES

Hand piecing, page 10

Partial seams, page 13

Adding borders, page 15

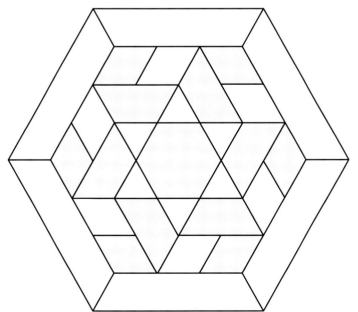

1. Make 6.

2. Join; make 2.

3. Make 1.

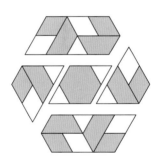

4. Join with partial seams.

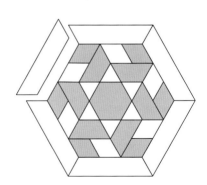

5. Join.

Summer Picnic

TECHNIQUES

Hand piecing, page 10

Adding borders, page 15

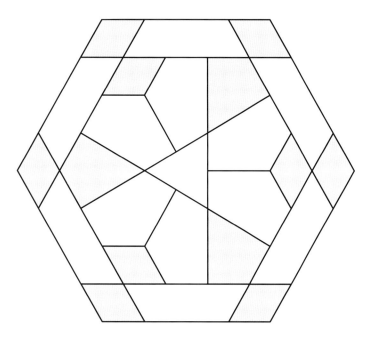

1. Make 3.

2. Make 2.

3. Make 1.

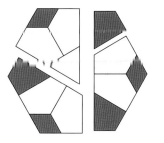

4. Join.

5. Join.

Rising Mist

TECHNIQUES

Hand piecing, page 10

Center stars, page 14

Adding borders, page 15

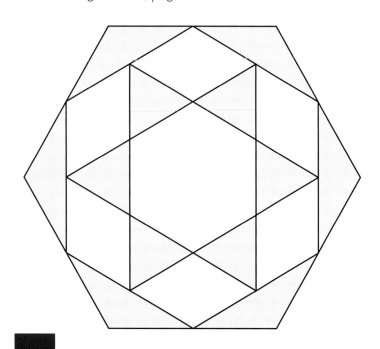

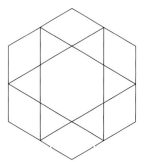

1. Make 1.

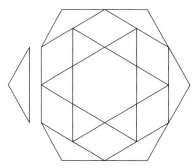

2. Join.

Spring Surprise

TECHNIQUES

Hand piecing, page 10

Center stars, page 14

Adding borders, page 15

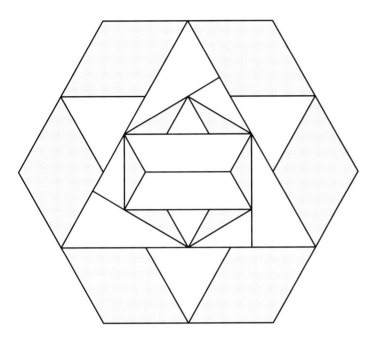

1. Make 1.

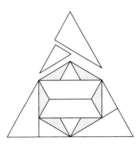

2. Join.

3. Make 3.

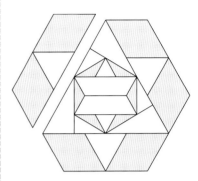

4. Join.

King of Versailles

TECHNIQUES

Hand piecing, page 10

Adding borders, page 15

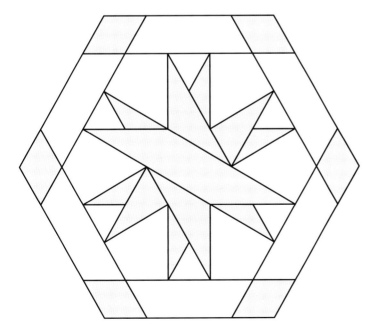

1. Make 4.

2. Make 2.

3. Make 2.

4. Join; make 2.

5. Make 1.

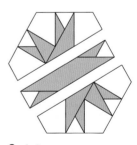

6. Join.

7. Join.

Portrait Pain

TECHNIQUES

Hand piecing, page 10

Adding borders, page 15

1. Make 3.

2. Make 3.

3. Make 3.

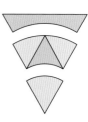

4. Make 3

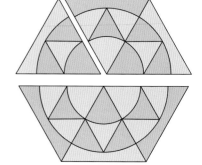

5. Join.

Sports Day

TECHNIQUES

Hand piecing, page 10

Adding borders, page 15

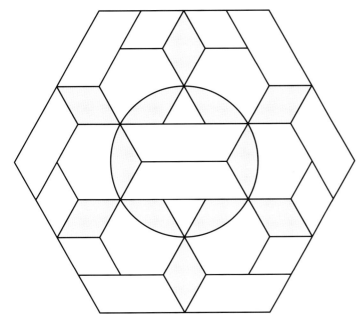

1. Make 3.

2. Make 3.

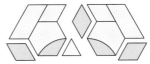

3. Join; make 1.

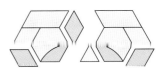

4. Join; make 1.

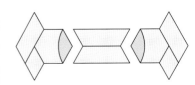

5. Join; make 1.

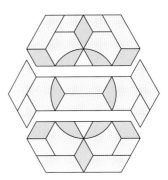

6. Join.

Childish Tube

TECHNIQUES

Hand piecing, page 10

Center stars, page 14

Adding borders, page 15

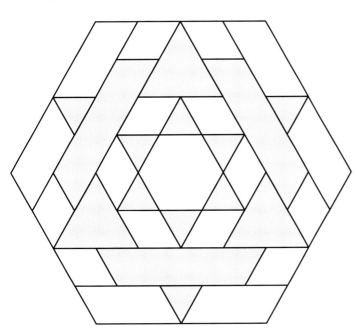

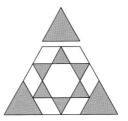

1. Join; make 1.

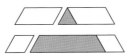

2. Make 3.

3. Join.

Rabbits in the Light

TECHNIQUES

Hand piecing, page 10

Adding borders, page 15

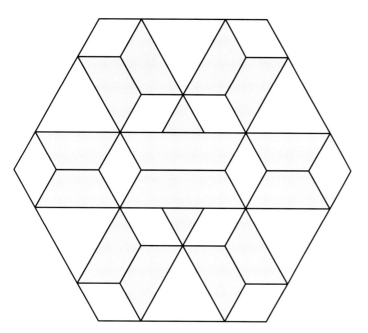

1. Make 6

2. Join; make 1.

3. Make 2.

4. Make 2.

5. Join; make 2.

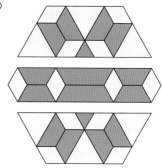

6. Join.

Accepted Few

TECHNIQUES

Hand piecing, page 10

Adding borders, page 15

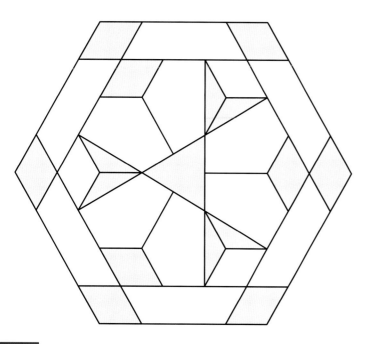

1. Make 3.

2. Make 3.

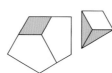

3. Make 2.

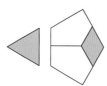

4. Make 1.

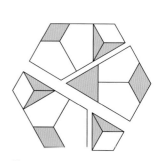

5. Join.

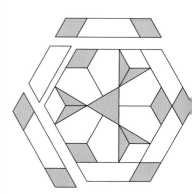

6. Join.

Denali

TECHNIQUES

Hand piecing, page 10

Adding borders, page 15

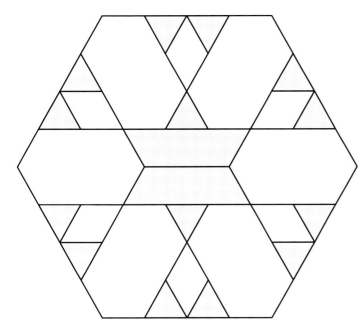

1. Make 6.

2. Make 2.

3. Make 2.

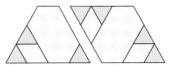

4. Join; make 2.

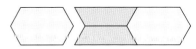

5. Make 1.

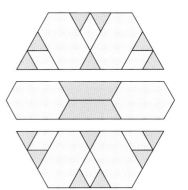

6. Join.

When Two Are One

TECHNIQUES

Appliqué, page 12

Trimming oversize blocks, page 13

Adding borders, page 15

Appliqué, using your preferred method.

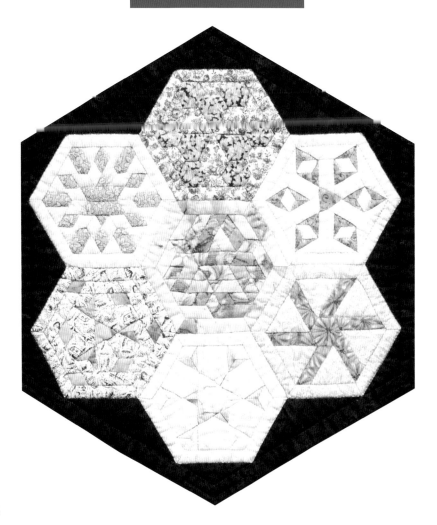

Twenty-One

TECHNIQUES

Hand piecing, page 10

Adding borders, page 15

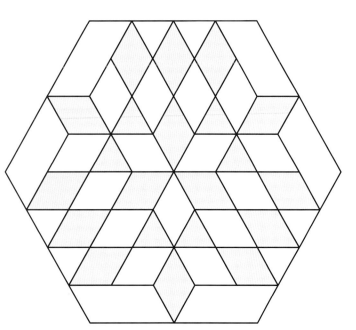

1. Make 3.

2. Make 3.

3. Join; make 1.

4. Join; make 1.

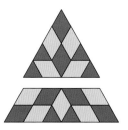

5. Join; make 1.

6. Make 3.

7. Join.

My Hero

TECHNIQUES

Hand piecing, page 10

Adding borders, page 15

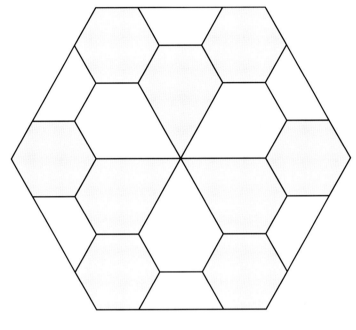

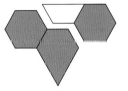

1. Make 3.

2. Make 2.

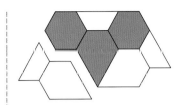

3. Make 1.

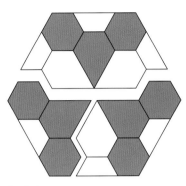

4. Join.

Salmon Run

TECHNIQUES

Hand piecing, page 10

Adding borders, page 15

1. Make 6.

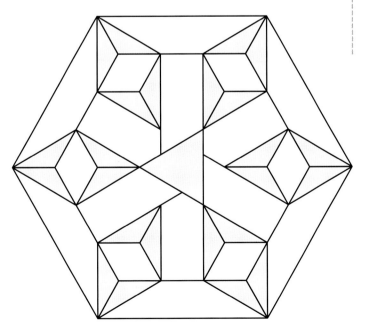

2. Make 3.

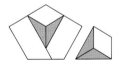

3. Join; make 2.

4. Make 1.

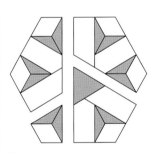

5. Join.

6. Make 6.

7. Join.

Fiesta

TECHNIQUES

Hand piecing, page 10

Adding borders, page 15

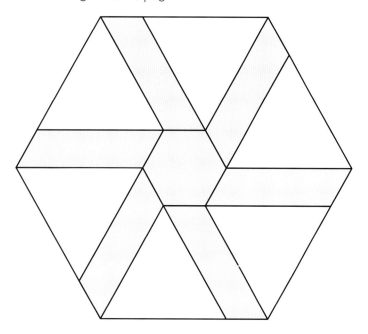

1. Make 6.

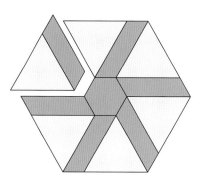

2. Join.

Rainbow Writing

TECHNIQUES

Hand piecing, page 10

Adding borders, page 15

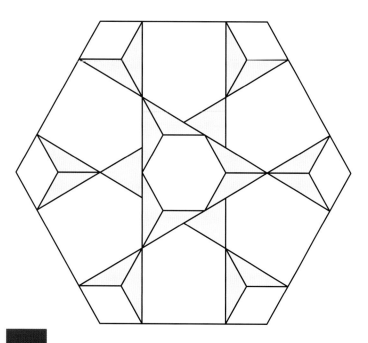

1. Make 6.

2. Make 5.

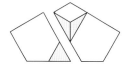

3. Join; make 3.

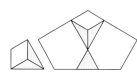

4. Join; make 2.

5. Join; make 1.

6. Make 1.

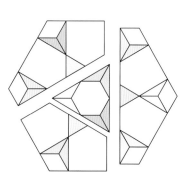

7. Join.

USA International

TECHNIQUES

Hand piecing, page 10

Adding borders, page 15

1. Make 3.

2. Make 3.

3. Join; make 2.

4. Make 1.

5. Join.

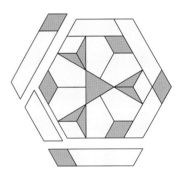

6. Join.

Sweet September

TECHNIQUES

Hand piecing, page 10

Adding borders, page 15

1. Make 6.

2. Make 2.

3. Join; make 2.

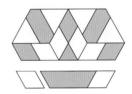

4. Join; make 2.

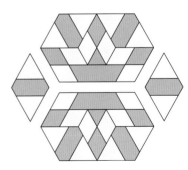

5. Join.

Mandola at Midnight

TECHNIQUES

Foundation piecing, page 11

Adding borders, page 15

1. Make 3 of each.

2. Sew A to B; make 3.

3. Sew C to D; make 3.

4. Sew triangle to CD unit; make 3.

5. Join.

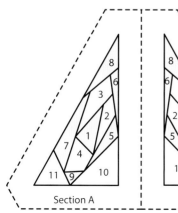

Section A

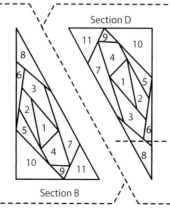

Section B

Section D

Section C

Tall Ships

TECHNIQUES

Foundation piecing, page 11

Adding borders, page 15

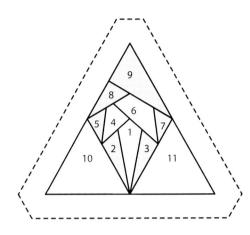

1. Make 6.

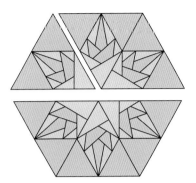

2. Join.

Winter Sun

TECHNIQUES

Hand piecing, page 10

Adding borders, page 15

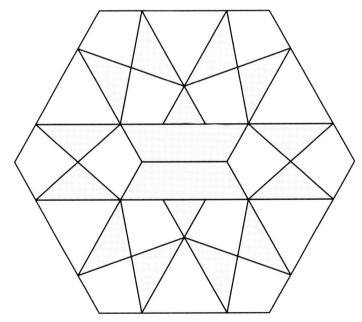

1. Make 6.

2. Join; make 1.

3. Make 2.

4. Make 2.

5. Join; make 2.

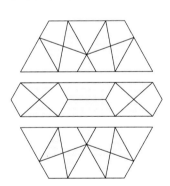

6. Join.

The Hunter's Web

TECHNIQUES

Foundation piecing, page 11

Adding borders, page 15

1. Make 3 of each.

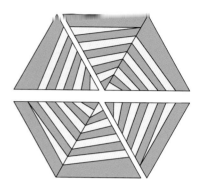

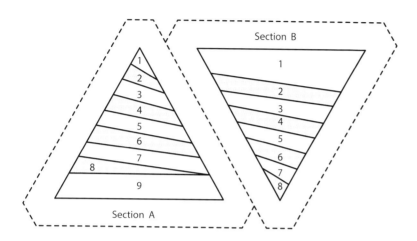

2. Alternating A and B, join.

The Rose Garden

TECHNIQUES

Hand piecing, page 10

Partial seams, page 13

Adding borders, page 15

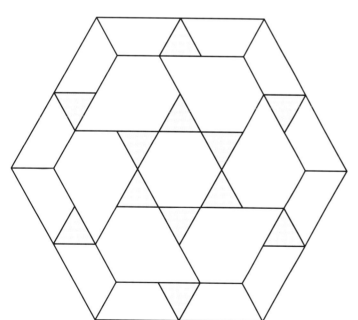

1. Make 6.

2. Join with partial seams.

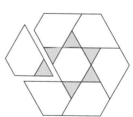

3. Join; complete the partial seam.

4. Make 6.

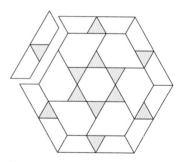

5. Join.

I'm Three

TECHNIQUES

Hand piecing, page 10

Adding borders, page 15

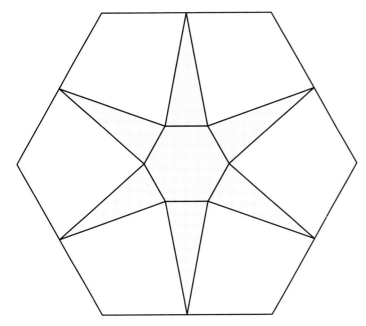

1. Make 2.

2. Make 2.

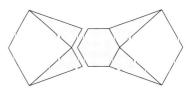

3. Join; make 1.

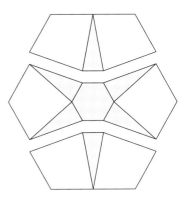

4. Join.

Sashiko Star

TECHNIQUES

Embroidery, page 12

Trimming oversize blocks, page 13

Adding borders, page 15

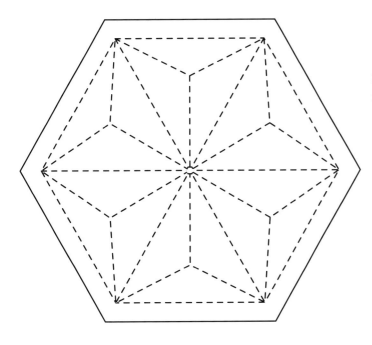

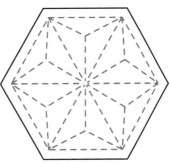

Stitch, using Olympus
Sashiko Thread, Purple 19.

Hidden Extras

TECHNIQUES

Hand piecing, page 10

Adding borders, page 15

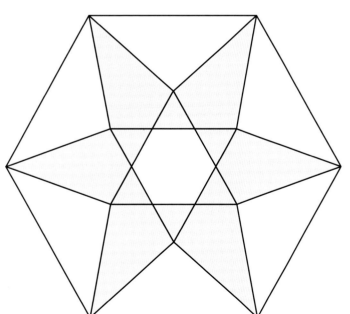

1. Make 4.

2. Make 2.

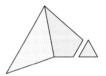

3. Make 2.

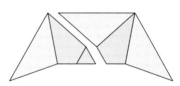

4. Join; make 2.

5. Make 1.

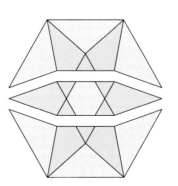

6. Join.

Watching

TECHNIQUES

Hand piecing, page 10

Foundation piecing, page 11

Adding borders, page 15

Sew together 1 light and 2 dark strips 1" × 7"; press the seam allowance outward.

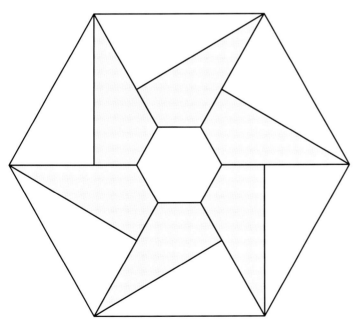

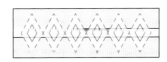

1. Center 6 templates on the strip; press and cut.

2. Make 6.

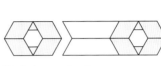

3. Join; make 1.

4. Make 2.

5. Join; make 2.

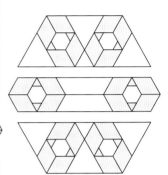

6. Join.

Turn Around

TECHNIQUES

Hand piecing, page 10

Adding borders, page 15

1. Make 6.

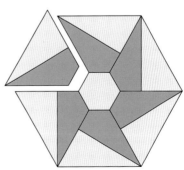

2. Join.

Sparrow's Flight

TECHNIQUES

Hand piecing, page 10

Adding borders, page 15

1. Make 3.

2. Make 3.

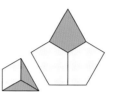

3. Join; make 2.

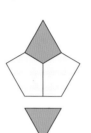

4. Make 1.

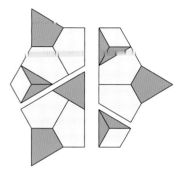

5. Join.

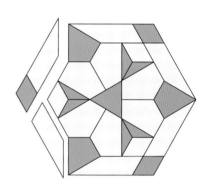

6. Join.

Relay for Life

TECHNIQUES

Hand piecing, page 10

Adding borders, page 15

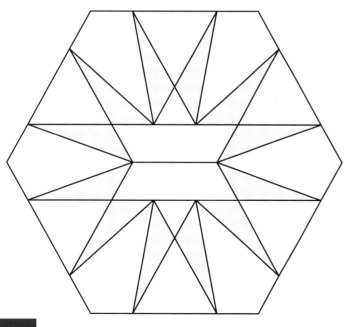

1. Make 6.

2. Join; make 1.

3. Make 2.

4. Join; make 2.

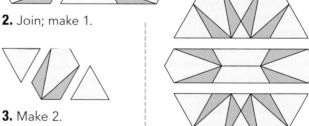

5. Join.

Lemon Soufflé

TECHNIQUES

Hand piecing, page 10

Adding borders, page 15

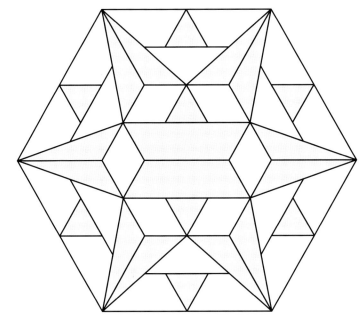

1. Make 6.

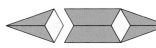

2. Join; make 1.

3. Make 6.

4. Join; make 2.

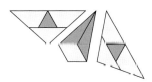

5. Join; make 2.

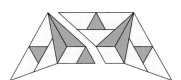

6. Join; make 2.

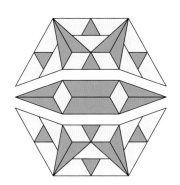

7. Join.

No Roses for Michael

TECHNIQUES

Hand piecing, page 10

Center stars, page 14

Adding borders, page 15

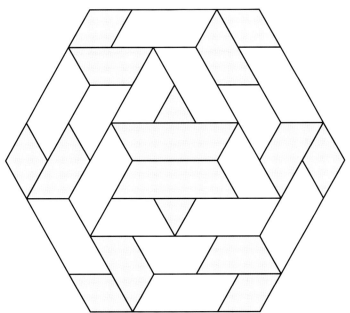

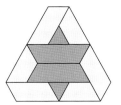

1. Make 1.

2. Make 3.

3. Make 3.

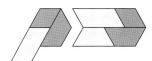

4. Join; make 3.

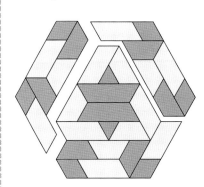

5. Join.

Log Cabin Baskets

TECHNIQUES

Foundation piecing, page 11

Adding borders, page 15

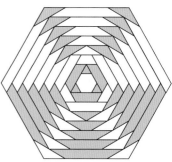

Make 1.

Maypole

TECHNIQUES

Hand piecing, page 10

Appliqué, page 12

Partial seams, page 13

Adding borders, page 15

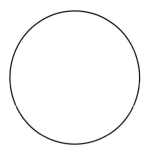

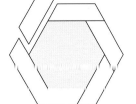

1. Join with a partial seam.

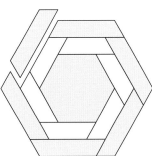

2. Join with a partial seam.

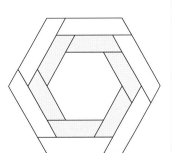

3. Repeat, reversing the colors.

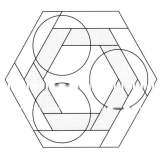

4. Cut 3 circles from second set, adding the seam allowance.

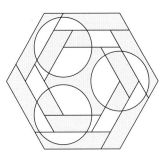

5. Appliqué the circles onto the first set.

Nature's Force

TECHNIQUES

Hand piecing, page 10

Adding borders, page 15

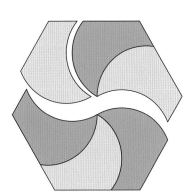

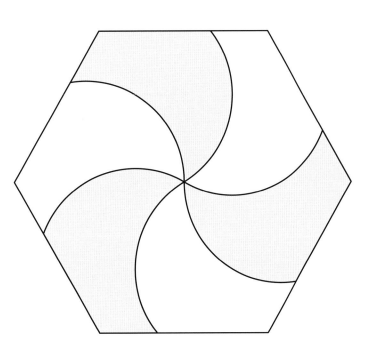

Join.

Spinning Spokes

TECHNIQUES

Hand piecing, page 10

Adding borders, page 15

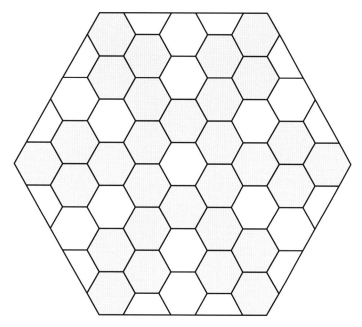

1. Make 6.

2. Make 6.

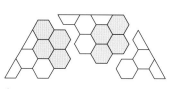

3. Join; make 2.

4. Make 1.

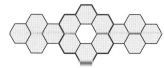

5. Join; make 1.

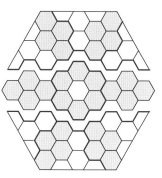

6. Join.

Argyle Sweaters

TECHNIQUES

Hand piecing, page 10

Adding borders, page 15

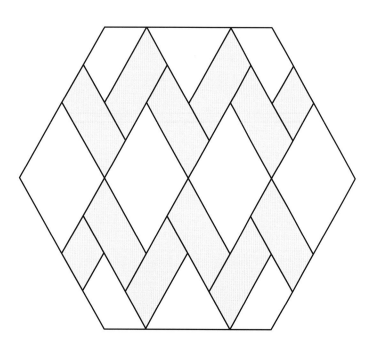

1. Make 2.

2. Join; make 1.

3. Join; make 1.

4. Make 2.

5. Join.

Norwegian Wind

TECHNIQUES

Hand piecing, page 10

Adding borders, page 15

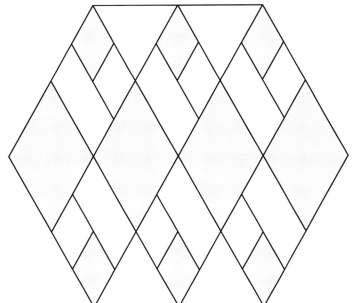

1. Make 6.

2. Join; make 4.

3. Make 2.

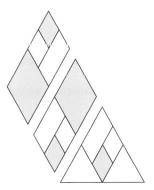

4. Join; make 2.

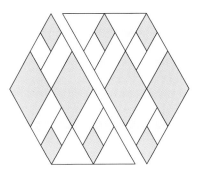

5. Join.

Winter Secrets

TECHNIQUES

Embroidery, page 12

Trimming oversize blocks, page 13

Adding borders, page 15

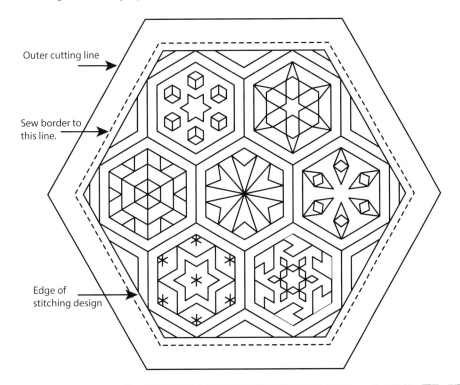

Outer cutting line

Sew border to this line.

Edge of stitching design

1. Stitch, using a single thread.

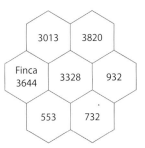

3013	3820	
Finca 3644	3328	932
	553	732

2. DMC thread colors; use DMC 3853 (Dark Autumn Gold / orange) for the outlines.

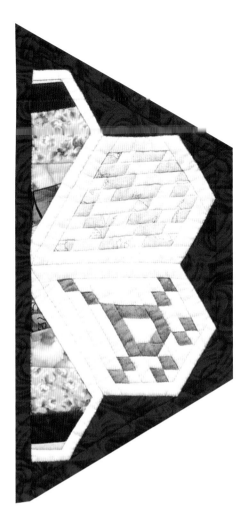

Pebbles in the Storm

TECHNIQUES

Foundation piecing, page 11

Adding borders, page 15

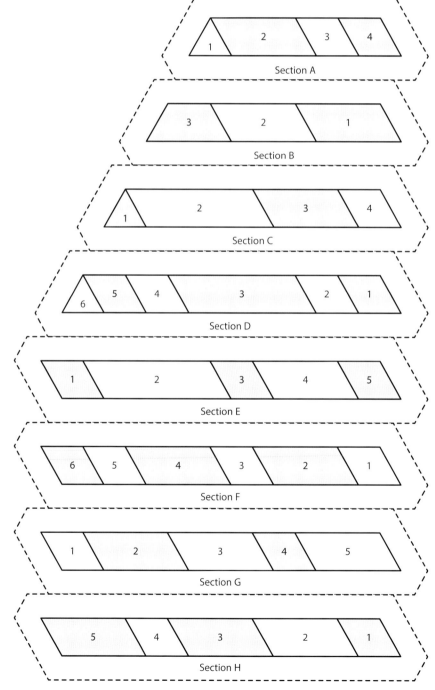

Section A

Section B

Section C

Section D

Section E

Section F

Section G

Section H

1. Make 1 of each.

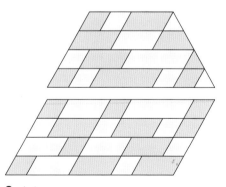

2. Join.

Cheryl's Pendant

TECHNIQUES

Foundation piecing, page 11

Adding borders, page 15

1. Make 1 of each.

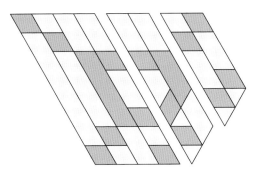

2. Join.

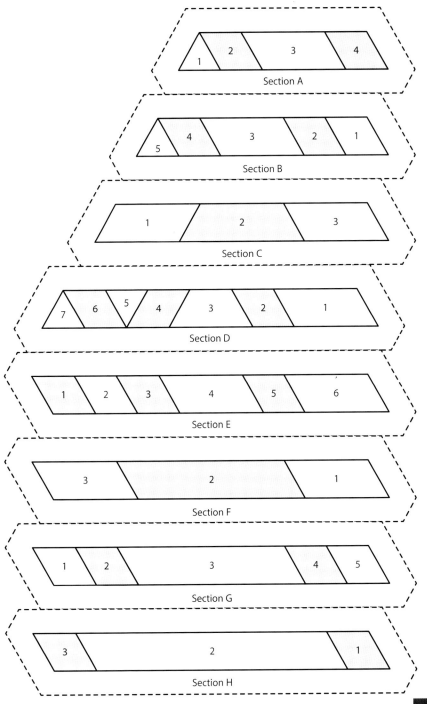

Section A

Section B

Section C

Section D

Section E

Section F

Section G

Section H

Searching

TECHNIQUES

Foundation piecing, page 11

Adding borders, page 15

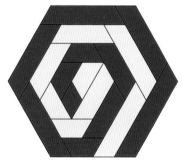

Make 1.

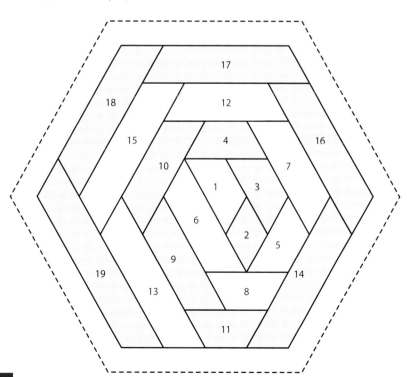

Goldilocks

TECHNIQUES

Foundation piecing, page 11

Adding borders, page 15

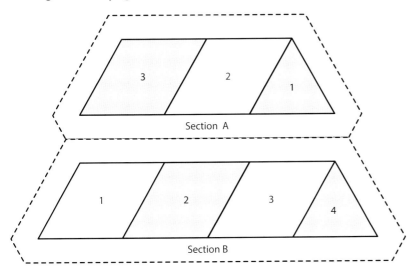

Section A

Section B

1. Make 2 of each.

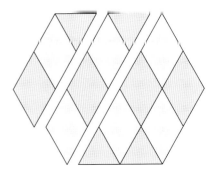

2. Join.

Bond Street

TECHNIQUES

Hand piecing, page 10

Partial seams, page 13

Adding borders, page 15

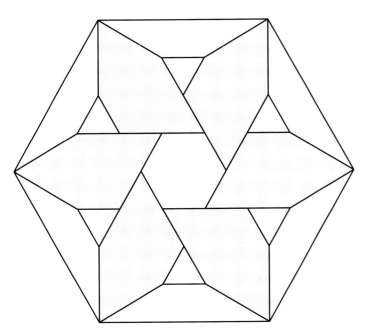

1. Make 6.

2. Join with a partial seam.

3. Join; complete the partial seam.

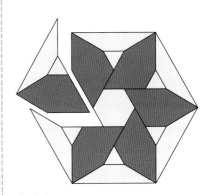

4. Join.

E. coli

TECHNIQUES

Hand piecing, page 10

Center stars, page 14

Adding borders, page 15

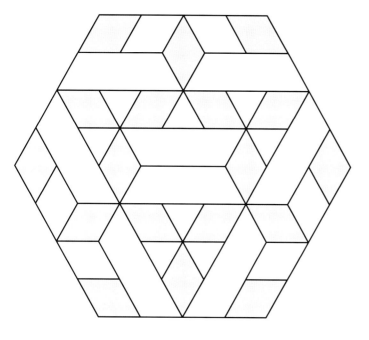

1. Make 1.

2. Make 3.

3. Make 3.

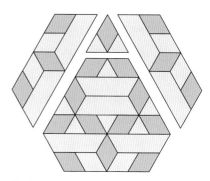

4. Join.

September

TECHNIQUES

Hand piecing, page 10

Adding borders, page 15

1. Make 6.

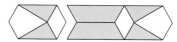

2. Join; make 1.

3. Make 2.

4. Make 2.

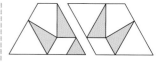

5. Join; make 2.

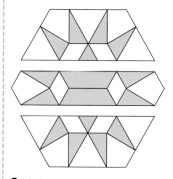

6. Join.

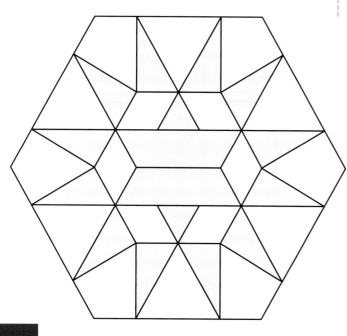

Bees to the Hive

TECHNIQUES

Hand piecing, page 10

Partial seams, page 13

Adding borders, page 15

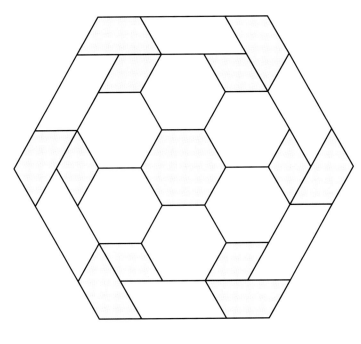

1. Make 1.

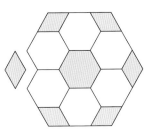

2. Join.

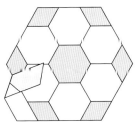

3. Join, using a partial seam.

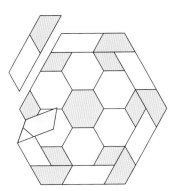

4. Join; complete the partial seam.

Enveloped

TECHNIQUES

Hand piecing, page 10

Center stars, page 14

Adding borders, page 15

1. Make 1.

2. Join.

3. Join; make 1.

4. Make 2.

5. Make 2.

6. Join; make 2.

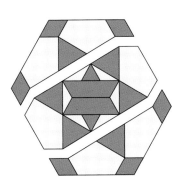

7. Join.

Still Too Small

TECHNIQUES

Hand piecing, page 10

Appliqué, page 12

Adding borders, page 15

1. Make 3.

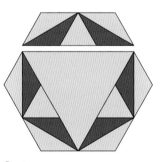

2. Join.

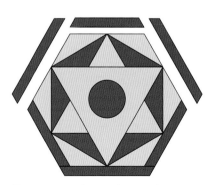

3. Join; appliqué the circle.

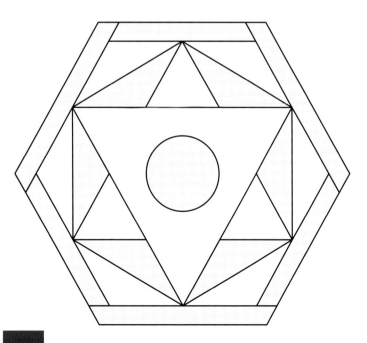

Yvonne's Mystery

TECHNIQUES

Foundation piecing, page 11

Trimming oversize blocks, page 13

Adding borders, page 15

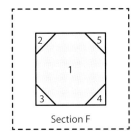

1. Make 1.

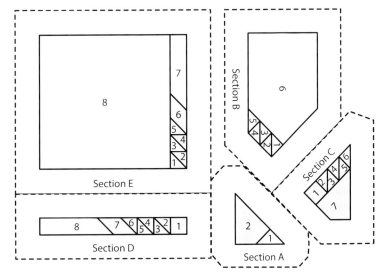

2. Make 4 of each.

3. Join E to D; make 4.

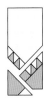

4. Join B to C and then BC to A; make 4.

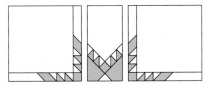

5. Join ED to ABC to ED; make 2.

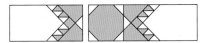

6. Join ABC to F to ABC; make 1.

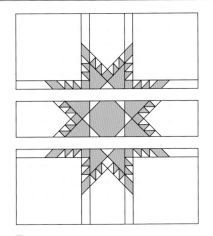

7. Join.

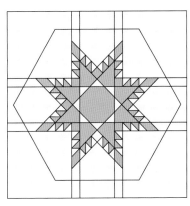

8. Trim.

Bull's Eye

TECHNIQUES

Appliqué, page 12

Adding borders, page 15

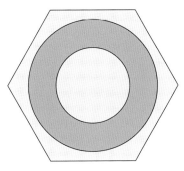

Appliqué, using your preferred method.

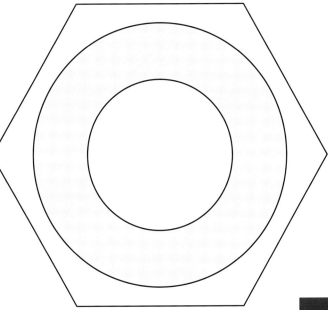

The Playpen

TECHNIQUES

Hand piecing, page 10

Adding borders, page 15

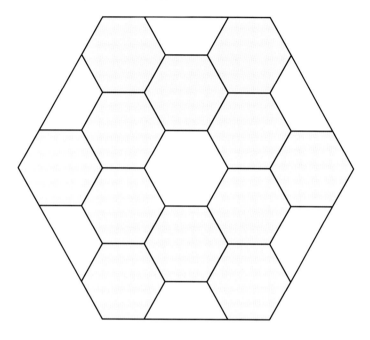

1. Make 1.

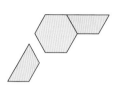

2. Make 3.

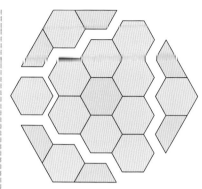

3. Join.

Tim Tam Spread

TECHNIQUES

Hand piecing, page 10

Adding borders, page 15

1. Make 6.

2. Join; make 1.

3. Make 2.

4. Make 2.

5. Join; make 2.

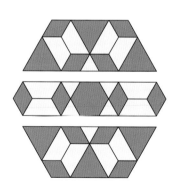

6. Join.

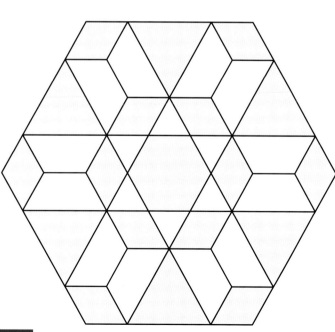

Ravishing Rhonda

TECHNIQUES

Hand piecing, page 10

Center stars, page 14

Adding borders, page 15

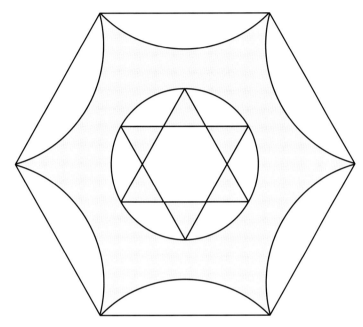

1. Make 1.

2. Join, or appliqué, if preferred.

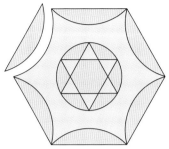

3. Join, or appliqué, if preferred.

Margaret's Choice

TECHNIQUES

Hand piecing, page 10

Center stars, page 14

Adding borders, page 15

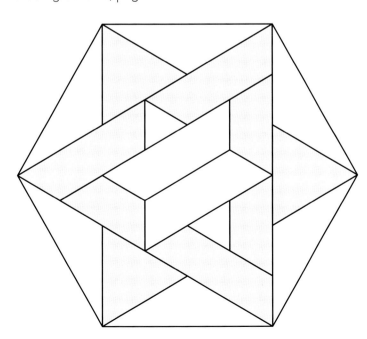

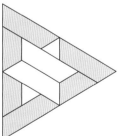

1. Make 1.

2. Make 3.

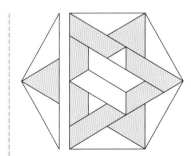

3. Join.

Fresh Start

TECHNIQUES

Hand piecing, page 10

Adding borders, page 15

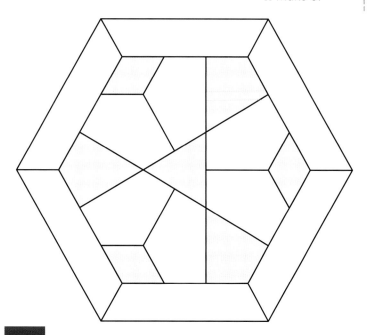

1. Make 3.

2. Make 2.

3. Make 1.

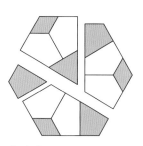

4. Join.

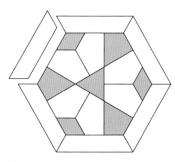

5. Join.

The Thief of Time

TECHNIQUES

Hand piecing, page 10

Adding borders, page 15

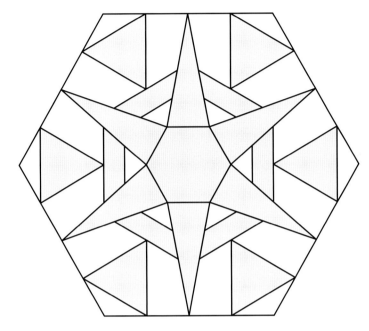

1. Make 6.

2. Make 6.

3. Join; make 2.

4. Make 2.

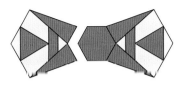

5. Join; make 1.

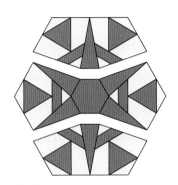

6. Join.

Scattered Jewels

TECHNIQUES

Hand piecing, page 10

Adding borders, page 15

1. Make 2.

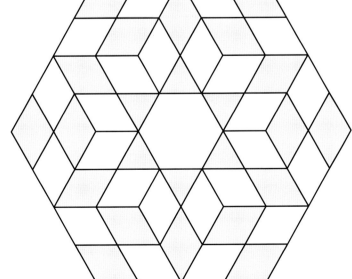

2. Make 6.

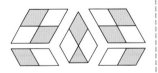

3. Join; make 2.

4. Make 2.

5. Join; make 1.

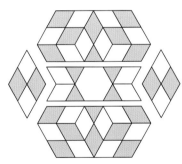

6. Join.

Gathering

TECHNIQUES

Hand piecing, page 10

Appliqué, page 12

Adding borders, page 15

1. Make 2.

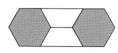

2. Join; make 1.

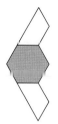

3. Make 2.

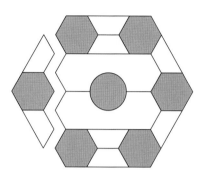

4. Join; appliqué the circle.

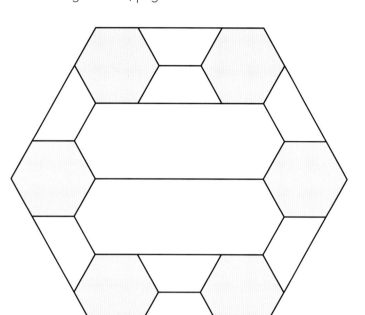

Dust 'n' Crumbs

TECHNIQUES

Foundation piecing, page 11

Adding borders, page 15

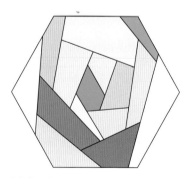

Make 1.

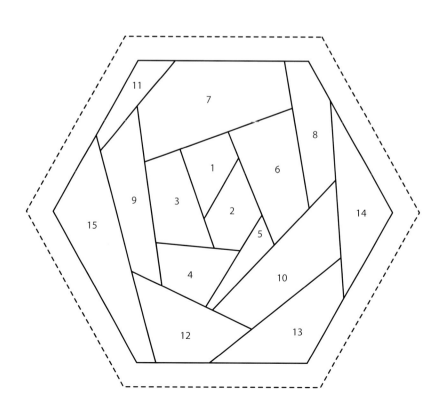

Pineapple Mixup

TECHNIQUES

Foundation piecing, page 11

Adding borders, page 15

Make 1.

Clover of Friendship

TECHNIQUES

Appliqué, page 12

Adding borders, page 15

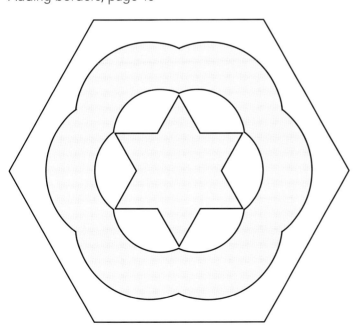

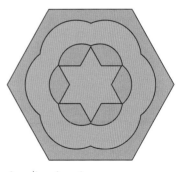

Appliqué, using your
preferred method.

Sunflowers

TECHNIQUES

Foundation piecing, page 11

Appliqué, page 12

Trimming oversize blocks, page 13

Adding borders, page 15

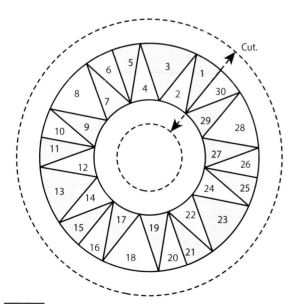

Cut.

1. Cut along all the dotted lines.

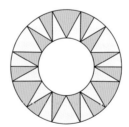

2. Make 1, and join the ends.

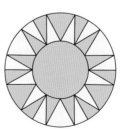

3. Stitch the circle into the center.

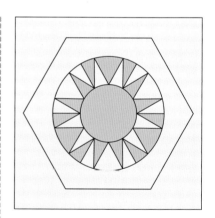

4. Appliqué to the center of a 6″ × 6″ square, and trim.

Louis XIV

TECHNIQUES

Hand piecing, page 10

Adding borders, page 15

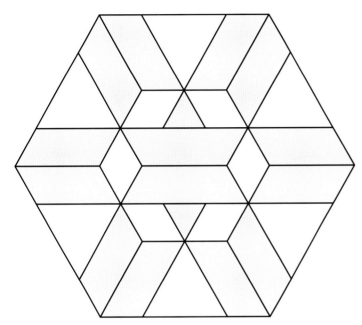

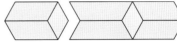

1. Make 6.

2. Join; make 1.

3. Make 2.

4. Make 2.

5. Join; make 2.

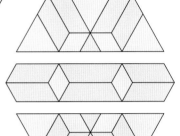

6. Join.

Hydrangeas

TECHNIQUES

Hand piecing, page 10

Adding borders, page 15

1. Make 6.

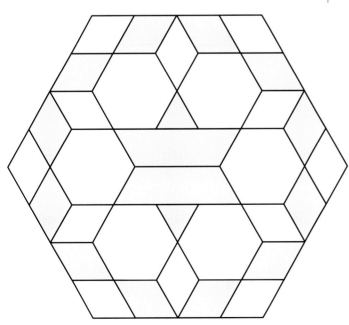

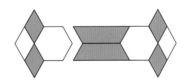

2. Join; make 1.

3. Make 2.

4. Make 2.

5. Join; make 2.

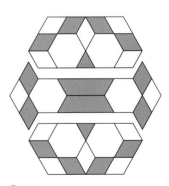

6. Join.

Writer's Lament

TECHNIQUES

Hand piecing, page 10

Adding borders, page 15

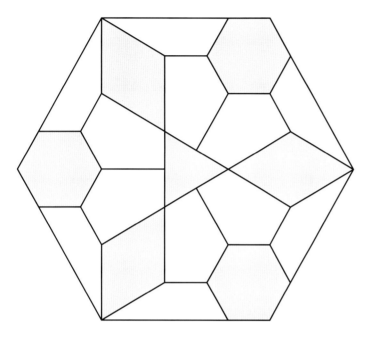

1. Make 3.

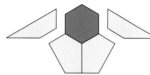

2. Make 3.

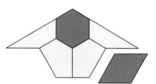

3. Make 2.

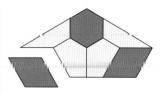

4. Make 1.

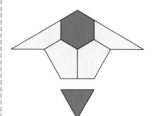

5. Make 1.

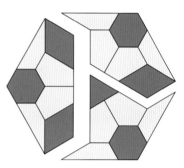

6. Join.

Jet Plane

TECHNIQUES

Hand piecing, page 10

Adding borders, page 15

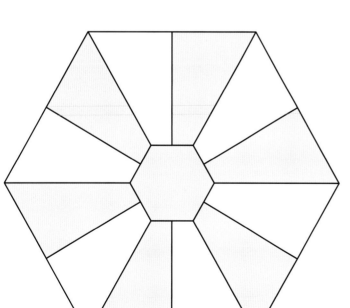

1. Make 6.

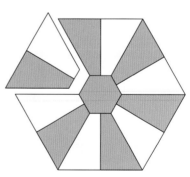

2. Join.

Evening Star

TECHNIQUES

Foundation piecing, page 11

Adding borders, page 15

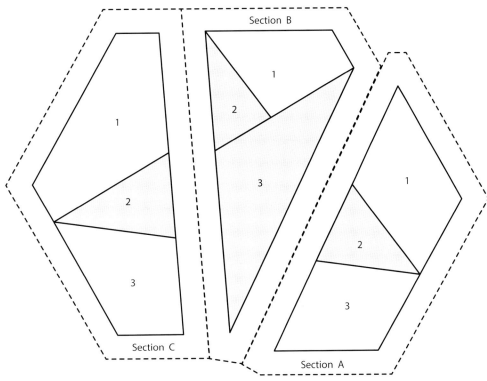

1. Make 1 of each.

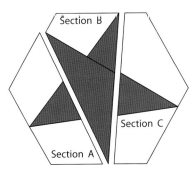

2. Join.

Flights of Fancy

TECHNIQUES

Hand piecing, page 10

Adding borders, page 15

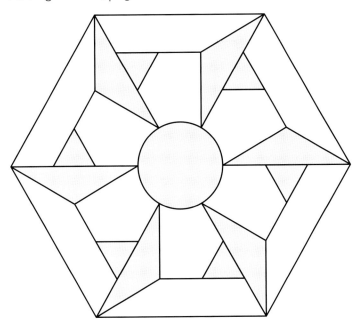

1. Make 6.

2. Make 6.

3. Join.

Secrets

TECHNIQUES

Foundation piecing, page 11

Adding borders, page 15

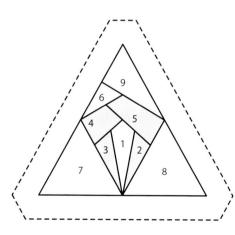

1. Make 6.

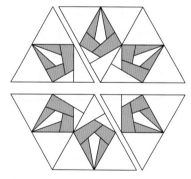

2. Join.

Place d'Italie

TECHNIQUES

Hand piecing, page 10

Adding borders, page 15

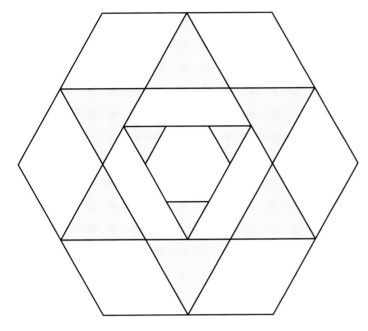

1. Make 1.

2. Make 1.

3. Make 3.

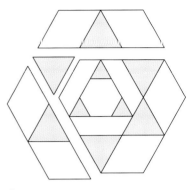

4. Join.

ToeNailsPaintedRed

TECHNIQUES

Hand piecing, page 10

Partial seams, page 13

Adding borders, page 15

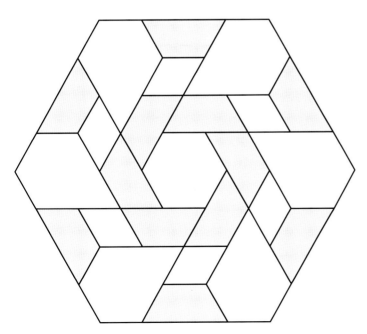

1. Make 6.

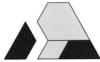

2. Join; make 6.

3. Join with a partial seam.

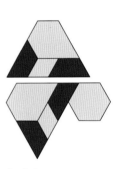

4. Join.

5. Join; complete the partial seam.

Peacock Green

TECHNIQUES

Hand piecing, page 10

Foundation piecing, page 11

Partial seams, page 13

Adding borders, page 15

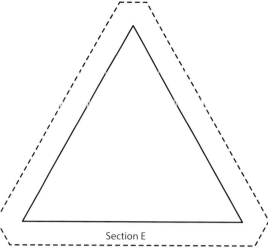

1. Cut 1.

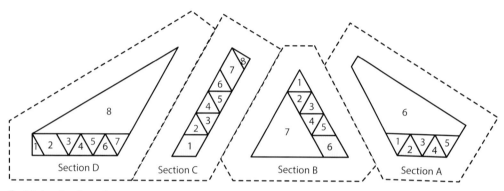

2. Make 3 of each.

3. Join A to B; make 3.

4. Join C to D; make 3.

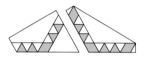

5. Join; make 3.

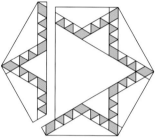

6. Join with a partial seam.

Eternal Hope

TECHNIQUES

Hand piecing, page 10

Partial seams, page 13

Adding borders, page 15

1. Make 6.

2. Make 6.

3. Join with a partial seam.

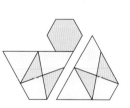

4. Join.

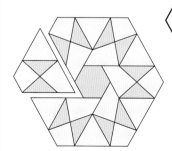

5. Join; complete the partial seam.

Frosted Windows

TECHNIQUES

Hand piecing, page 10

Adding borders, page 15

1. Make 3.

2. Make 2.

3. Make 1.

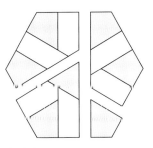

4. Join.

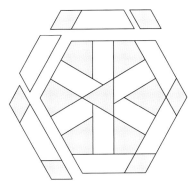

5. Join.

Beans Please

TECHNIQUES

Hand piecing, page 10

Adding borders, page 15

1. Make 6.

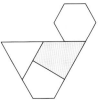

2. Join.

3. Join.

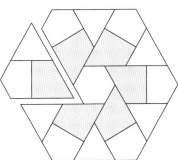

4. Join.

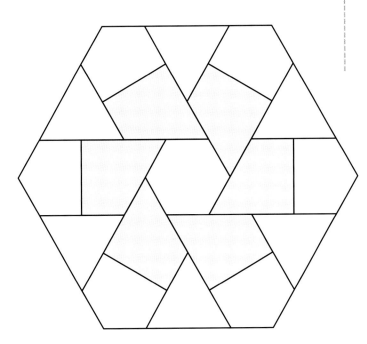

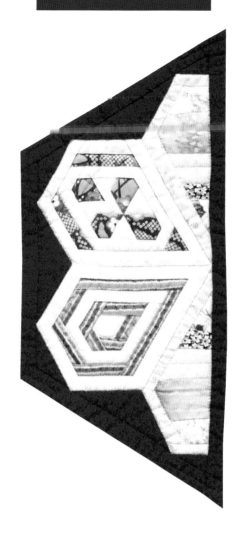

Downsizing the Ego

TECHNIQUES

Foundation piecing, page 11

Adding borders, page 15

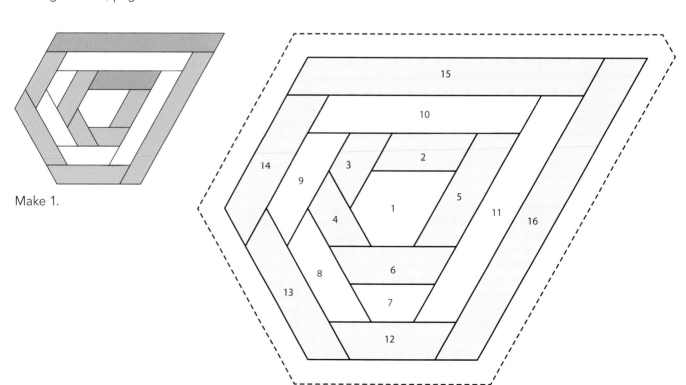

Make 1.

Friend or Foe

TECHNIQUES

Hand piecing, page 10

Adding borders, page 15

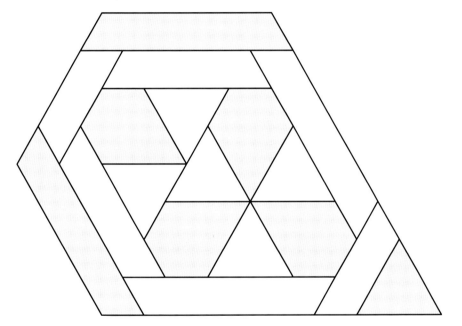

1. Make 2.

2. Make 1.

3. Join.

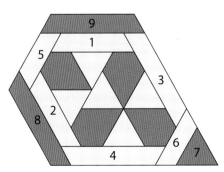

4. Join in the numbered sequence.

Winter Grace

TECHNIQUES

Appliqué, page 12

Adding borders, page 15

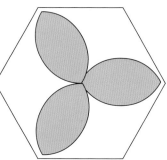

1. Appliqué, using your preferred method.

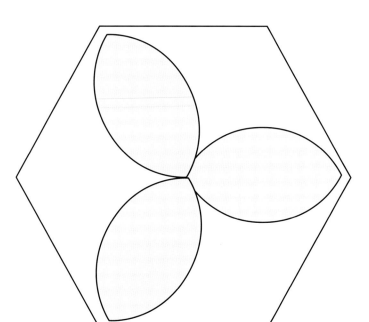

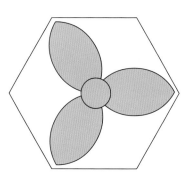

2. Appliqué the circle.

Too Thin

TECHNIQUES

Hand piecing, page 10

Center stars, page 14

Adding borders, page 15

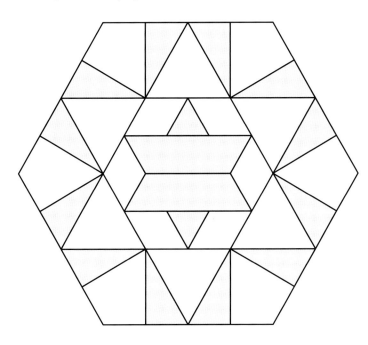

1. Make 1.

2. Make 6.

3. Make 3.

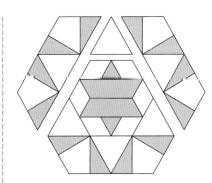

4. Join.

Merry Stitchers

TECHNIQUES

Foundation piecing, page 11

Adding borders, page 15

Make 1.

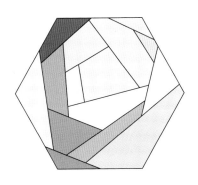

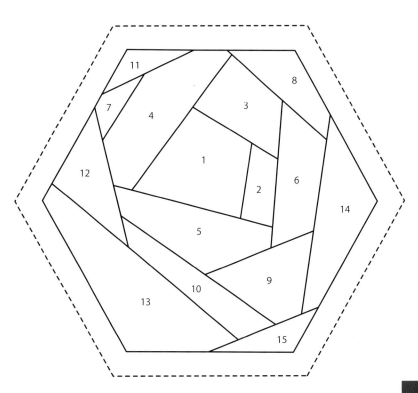

Whirling Wind

TECHNIQUES

Hand piecing, page 10

Adding borders, page 15

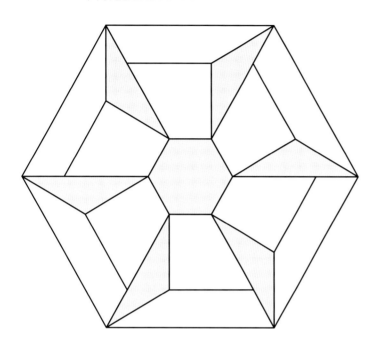

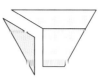

1. Make 6.

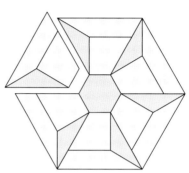

2. Join.

Remembering

TECHNIQUES

Hand piecing, page 10

Adding borders, page 15

Cut a 1½˝ × 2˝ strip from both fabrics and join on long edge.

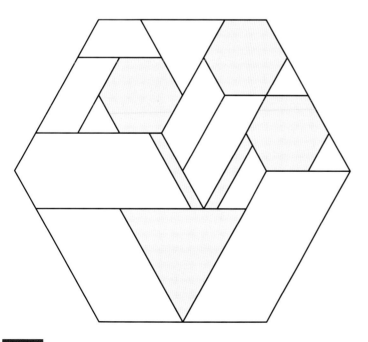

1. Cut from joined strips; make 1.

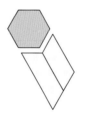

2. Join; make 1.

3. Join.

4. Make 1.

5. Join.

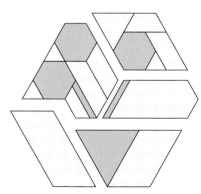

6. Join.

The Date

TECHNIQUES

Hand piecing, page 10

Adding borders, page 15

1. Make 6

2. Join; make 1

5. Join; make 2.

3. Make 2.

4. Make 2.

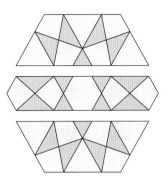

6. Join.

Through the Lattice

TECHNIQUES

Hand piecing, page 10

Adding borders, page 15

1. Make 3.

2. Make 3.

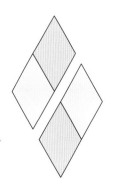

3. Make 1.

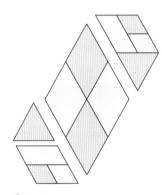

4. Join.

5. Join; make 2.

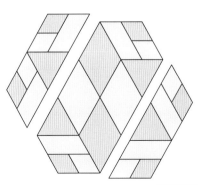

6. Join.

The Future Awaits

TECHNIQUES

Foundation piecing, page 11

Adding borders, page 15

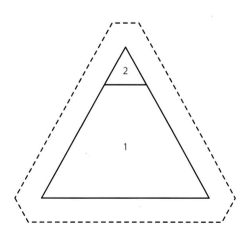

1. Make 6.

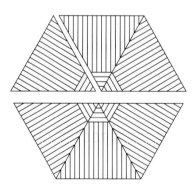

2. Join.

Coming Together

TECHNIQUES

Hand piecing, page 10

Adding borders, page 15

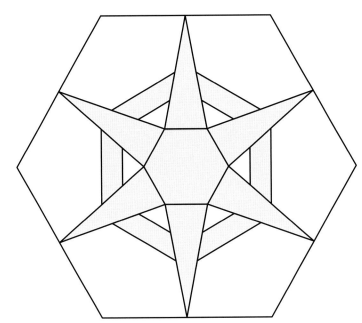

1. Make 6.

2. Join; make 2.

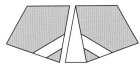

3. Make 2.

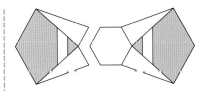

4. Join; make 1.

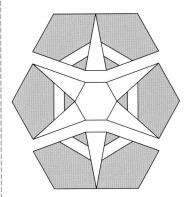

5. Join.

Ribbons of Peace

TECHNIQUES

Hand piecing, page 10

Center stars, page 14

Adding borders, page 15

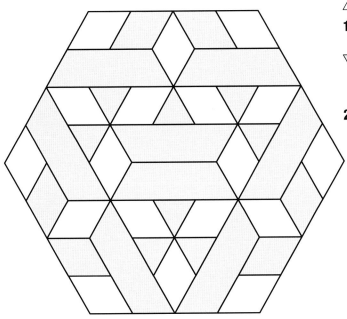

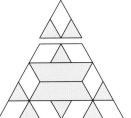

1. Make 1; join.

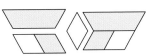

2. Make 3.

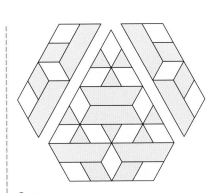

3. Join.

Isobel's Flight

TECHNIQUES

Foundation piecing, page 11

Adding borders, page 15

1. Make 2 of each.

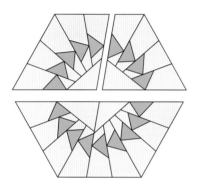

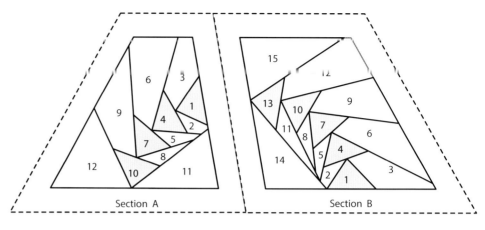

Section A

Section B

2. Join.

Size Irrelevant

TECHNIQUES

Foundation piecing, page 11

Adding borders, page 15

1. Make 1 of each.

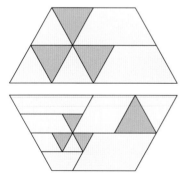

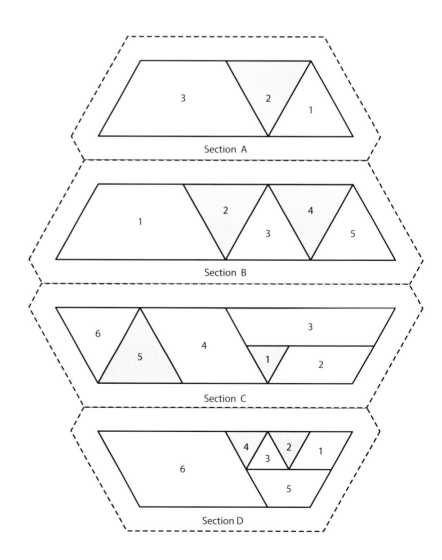

Section A

Section B

Section C

Section D

2. Join.

Looking for Gems

TECHNIQUES

Hand piecing, page 10

Center stars, page 14

Adding borders, page 15

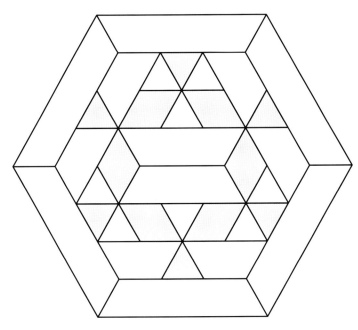

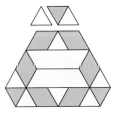

1. Make 1; join.

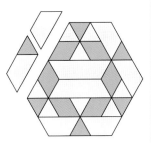

2. Join.

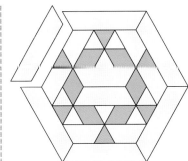

3. Join.

Rhonda Loves Spots

TECHNIQUES

Foundation piecing, page 11

Adding borders, page 15

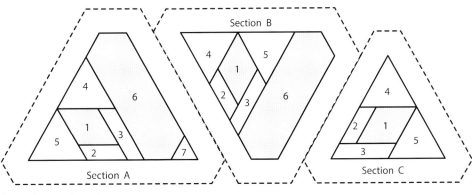

Section B

Section A

Section C

1. Make 2 of each.

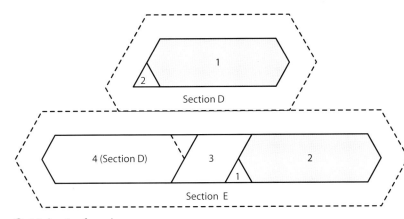

Section D

Section E

2. Make 1 of each.

3. Join A to B to C; make 2.

4. Join D to E; make 1.

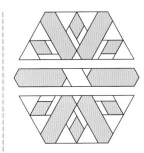

5. Join.

Lime Sundae

TECHNIQUES

Hand piecing, page 10

Center stars, page 14

Adding borders, page 15

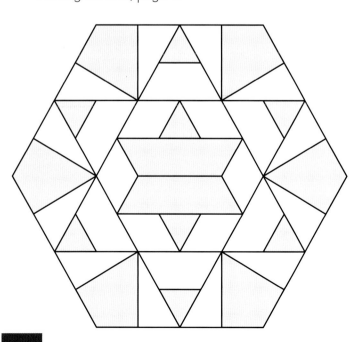

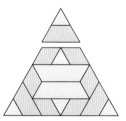

1. Make 1; join.

2. Make 6.

3. Make 3.

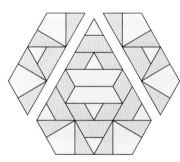

4. Join.

Pop!

TECHNIQUES

Hand piecing, page 10

Partial seams, page 13

Adding borders, page 15

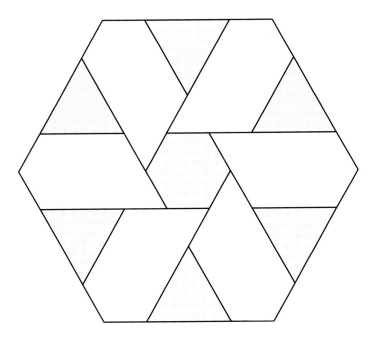

1. Make 6.

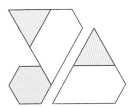

2. Join with a partial seam.

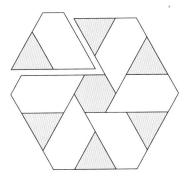

3. Join; complete the partial seam.

Whirling Too

TECHNIQUES

Hand piecing, page 10

Adding borders, page 15

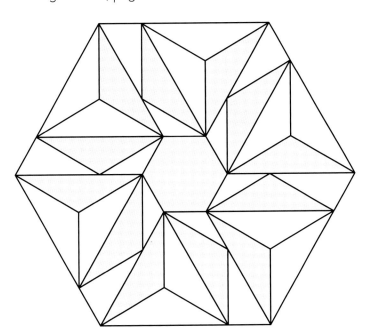

1. Make 6.

2. Make 6.

3. Join; make 6.

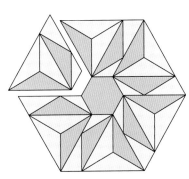

4. Join.

Cotton Spice

TECHNIQUES

Hand piecing, page 10

Center stars, page 14

Adding borders, page 15

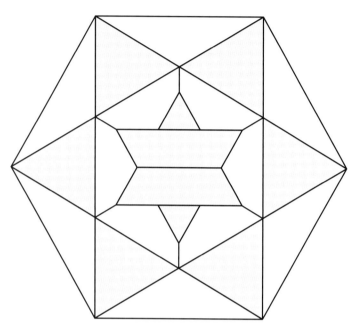

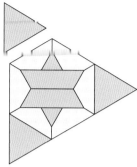

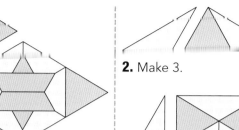

2. Make 3.

1. Make 1; join.

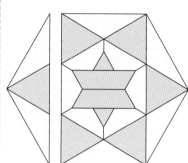

3. Join.

Sweet Caress

TECHNIQUES

Hand piecing, page 10

Adding borders, page 15

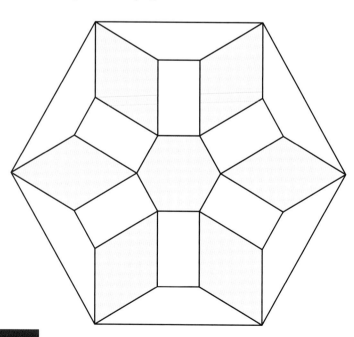

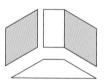

1. Make 3.

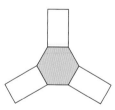

2. Make 1.

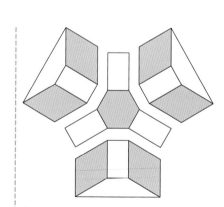

3. Join.

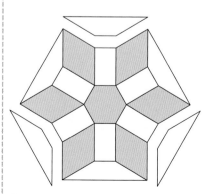

4. Join.

Flowing Ribbons

TECHNIQUES

Hand piecing, page 10

Adding borders, page 15

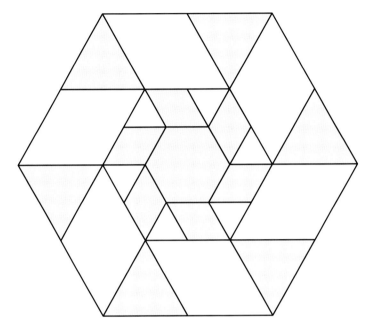

1. Make 6.

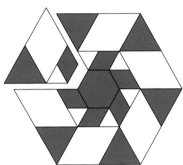

2. Join.

Itsy Bitsy

TECHNIQUES

Hand piecing, page 10

Center stars, page 14

Adding borders, page 15

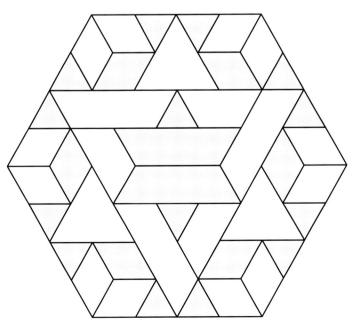

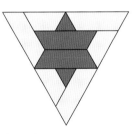

1. Make 1.

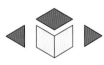

2. Make 6.

3. Join; make 3.

4. Join.

Planes of Paper

TECHNIQUES

Hand piecing, page 10

Adding borders, page 15

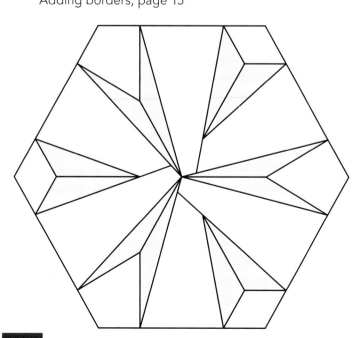

1. Make 3.

2. Join; make 3.

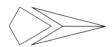

3. Make 3.

4. Join; make 3.

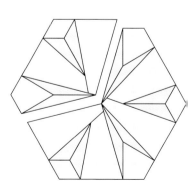

5. Join.

Ribbons Aflutter

TECHNIQUES

Hand piecing, page 10

Adding borders, page 15

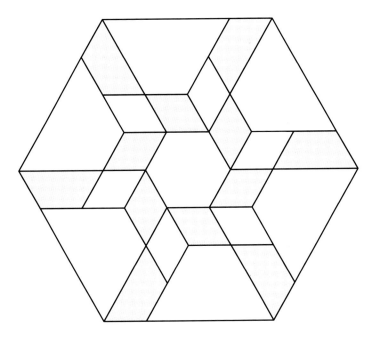

1. Make 6.

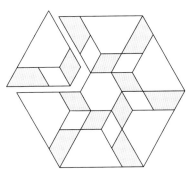

2. Join.

Psychedelic Swirl

TECHNIQUES

Hand piecing, page 10

Adding borders, page 15

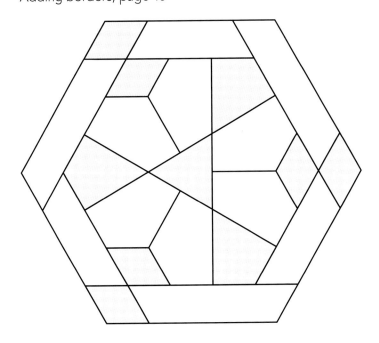

1. Make 3.

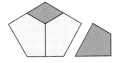

2. Join; make 2.

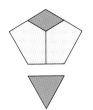

3. Join; make 1.

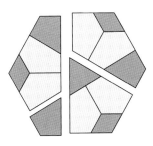

4. Join.

5. Join.

Ouch!

TECHNIQUES

Hand piecing, page 10

Center stars, page 14

Adding borders, page 15

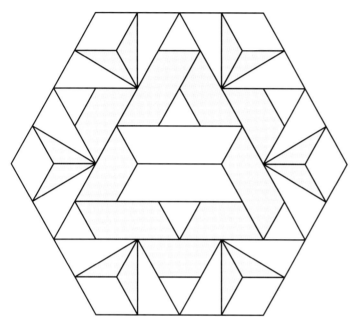

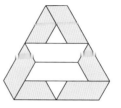

1. Make 1.

2. Make 6.

3. Join; make 6.

4. Join; make 3.

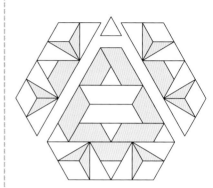

5. Join.

Good Morning

TECHNIQUES

Hand piecing, page 10

Adding borders, page 15

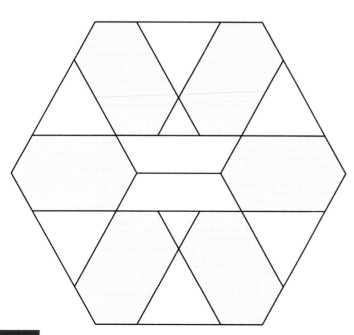

1. Make 2.

2. Make 2.

3. Join; make 2.

4. Make 1.

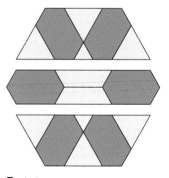

5. Join.

Too Tight

TECHNIQUES

Hand piecing, page 10

Center stars, page 14

Adding borders, page 15

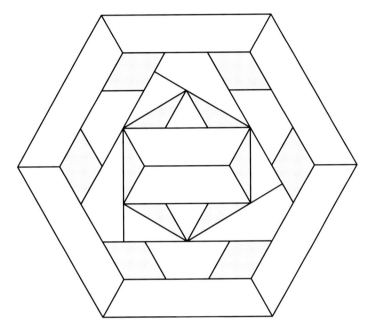

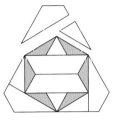

1. Make 1; join.

2. Make 3.

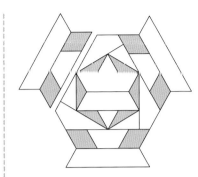

3. Join.

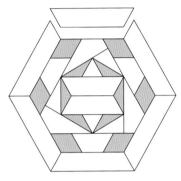

4. Join.

Bali Jungle

TECHNIQUES

Hand piecing, page 10

Partial seams, page 13

Adding borders, page 15

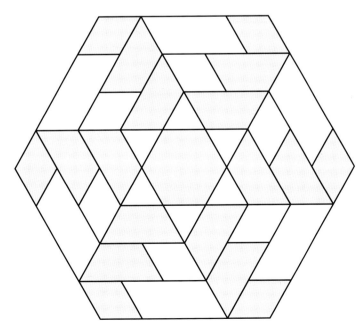

1. Make 6.

2. Make 4.

3. Join; make 2.

4. Make 1.

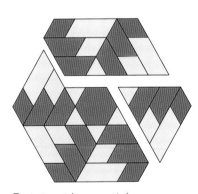

5. Join with a partial seam.

Fairy on a Stick

TECHNIQUES

Hand piecing, page 10

Adding borders, page 15

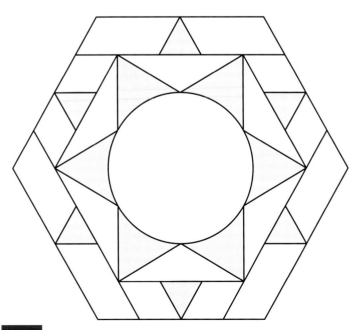

1. Make 3.

2. Make 3.

3. Join.

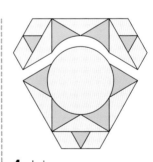

4. Join.

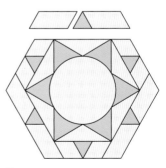

5. Join.

Kimberley Gem

TECHNIQUES

Hand piecing, page 10

Partial seams, page 13

Adding borders, page 15

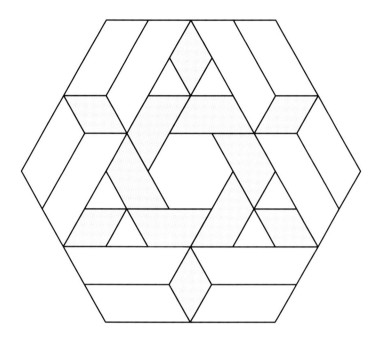

1. Join with a partial seam.

2. Join.

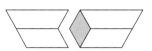

3. Join; make 3.

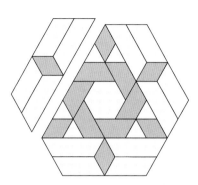

4. Join.

Occidental

TECHNIQUES

Hand piecing, page 10

Adding borders, page 15

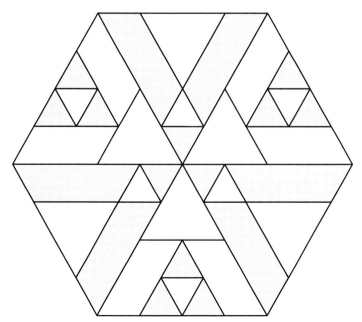

1. Make 3.

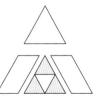

2. Join; make 3.

3. Make 3.

4. Join.

Sparrow's Flight Too

TECHNIQUES

Hand piecing, page 10

Adding borders, page 15

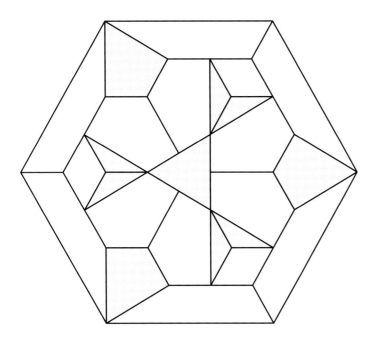

1. Make 3.

2. Make 3.

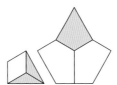

3. Join; make 2.

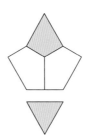

4. Make 1.

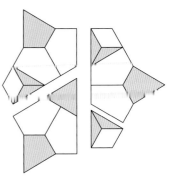

5. Join.

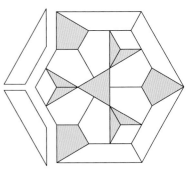

6. Join.

Kanuka

TECHNIQUES

Hand piecing, page 10

Adding borders, page 15

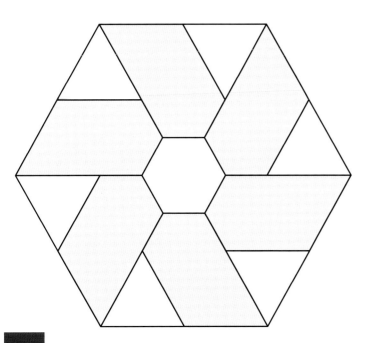

1. Make 6.

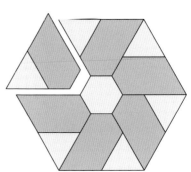

2. Join.

Space Invaders

TECHNIQUES

Hand piecing, page 10

Adding borders, page 15

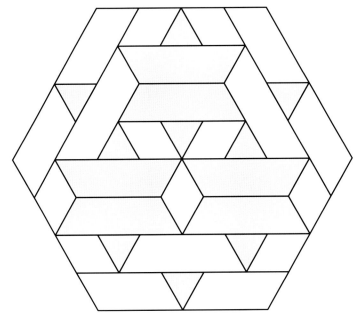

1. Make 1.

2. Make 1.

3. Join.

4. Make 1.

5. Make 1.

6. Join.

Windmills of Dust

TECHNIQUES

Hand piecing, page 10

Adding borders, page 15

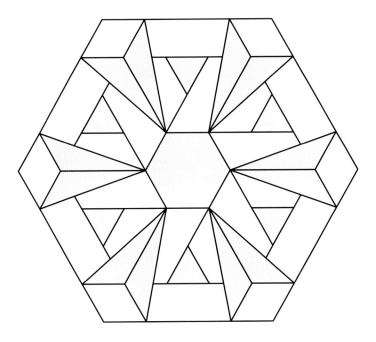

1. Make 6.

2. Make 6.

3. Join; make 2.

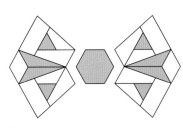

4. Join; make 1.

5. Join; make 2.

6. Join.

Petals in the Stream

TECHNIQUES

Hand piecing, page 10

Adding borders, page 15

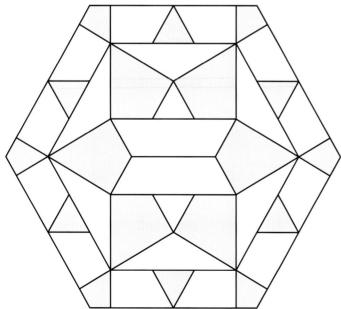

1. Make 2.

2. Make 2.

3. Make 2.

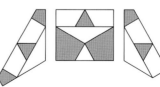

4. Make 2.

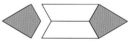

5. Join.

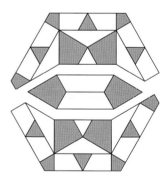

6. Join.

Up or Down?

TECHNIQUES

Hand piecing, page 10

Adding borders, page 15

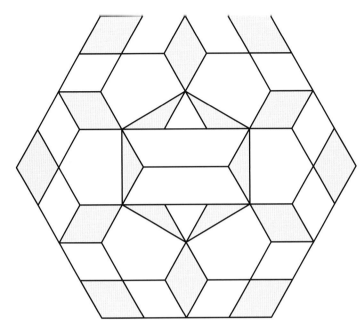

1 Make 1

2. Make 6.

3. Join; make 1.

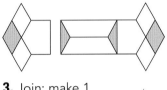

4. Make 2.

5. Make 2.

6. Join; make 2.

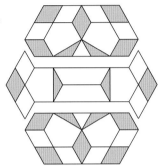

7. Join.

Penny Lane

TECHNIQUES

Hand piecing, page 10

Center stars, page 14

Adding borders, page 15

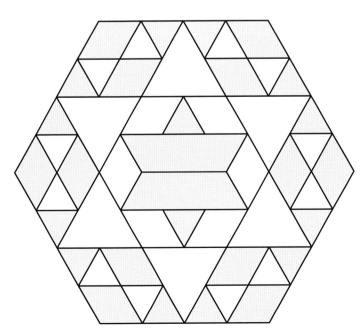

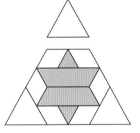

1. Make 1; join.

2. Make 6.

3. Make 3.

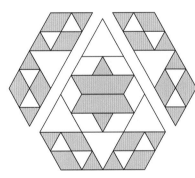

4. Join.

Consternation

TECHNIQUES

Hand piecing, page 10

Adding borders, page 15

1. Make 3.

2. Join; make 3.

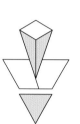

3. Join; make 2.

4. Join; make 1.

5. Join.

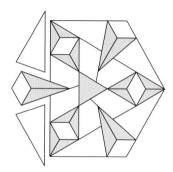

6. Join.

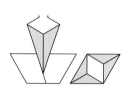

Castle Keep

TECHNIQUES

Hand piecing, page 10

Partial seams, page 13

Adding borders, page 15

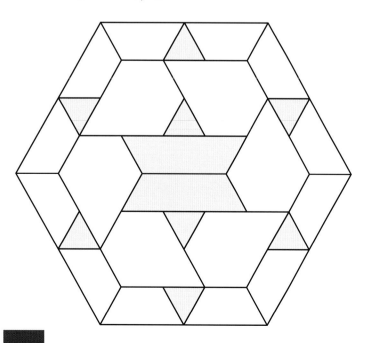

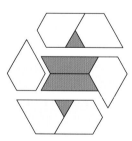

1. Make 2.

2. Join with a partial seam.

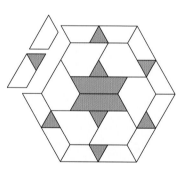

3. Join.

Debutante Ball

TECHNIQUES

Hand piecing, page 10

Adding borders, page 15

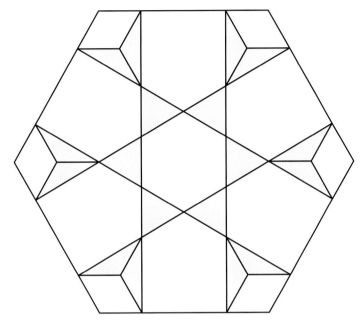

1. Make 1.

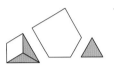

2. Make 6.

3. Make 2.

4. Make 2.

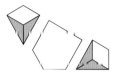

5. Join; make 2.

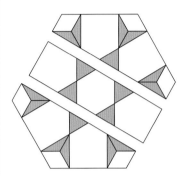

6. Join.

Spring Blossoms

TECHNIQUES

Hand piecing, page 10

Adding borders, page 15

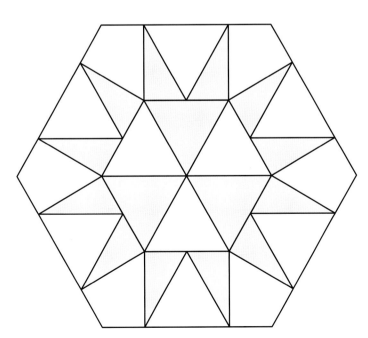

1. Make 6.

2. Join; make 3.

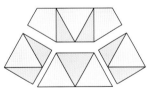

3. Join.

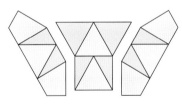

4. Join.

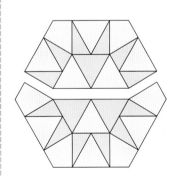

5. Join.

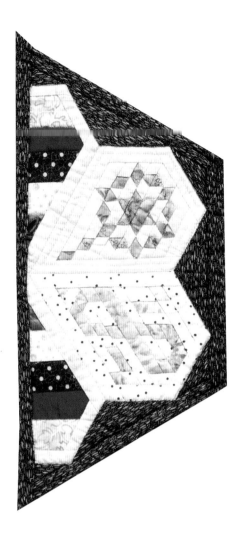

Melitta's Star

TECHNIQUES

Foundation piecing, page 11

Adding borders, page 15

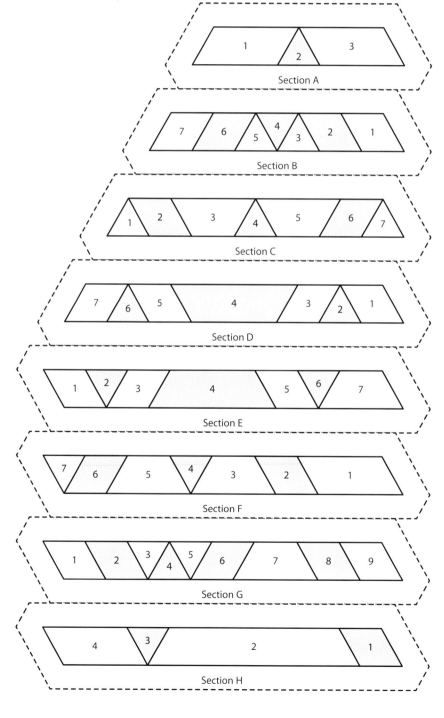

Section A

Section B

Section C

Section D

Section E

Section F

Section G

Section H

1. Make 1 of each.

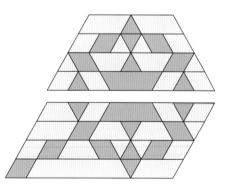

2. Join.

Always Hopeful

TECHNIQUES

Foundation piecing, page 11

Adding borders, page 15

1. Make 1 of each.

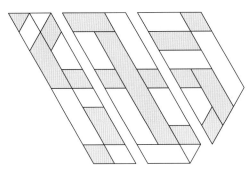

2. Join.

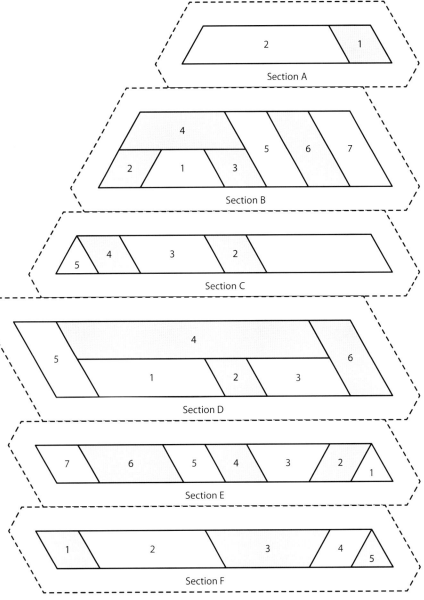

Section A

Section B

Section C

Section D

Section E

Section F

Bursting Out

TECHNIQUES

Hand piecing, page 10

Adding borders, page 15

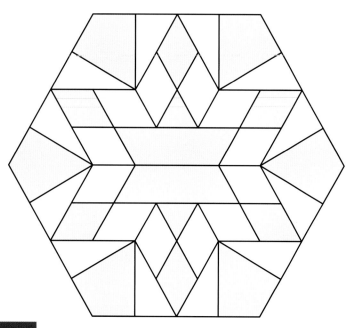

1. Make 2.

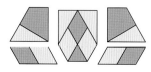

2. Join; make 2.

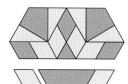

3. Join; make 2.

4. Make 2.

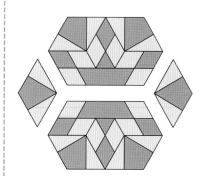

5. Join.

Trifids

TECHNIQUES

Hand piecing, page 10

Adding borders, page 15

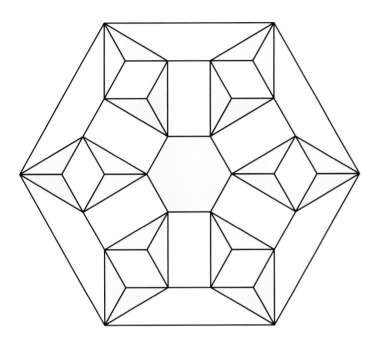

1. Make 6.

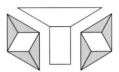

2. Join; make 3.

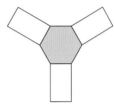

3. Make 1.

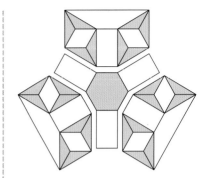

4. Join.

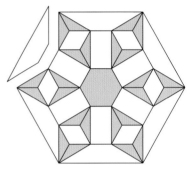

5. Join.

The Beat Goes On

TECHNIQUES

Hand piecing, page 10

Adding borders, page 15

1. Make 6.

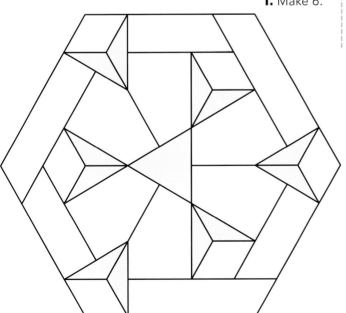

2. Make 3.

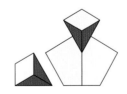

3. Join; make 2.

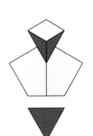

4. Join; make 1.

5. Join.

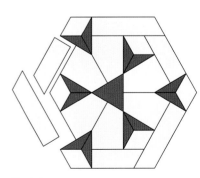

6. Join.

The Lotus

TECHNIQUES

Hand piecing, page 10

Appliqué, page 12

Adding borders, page 15

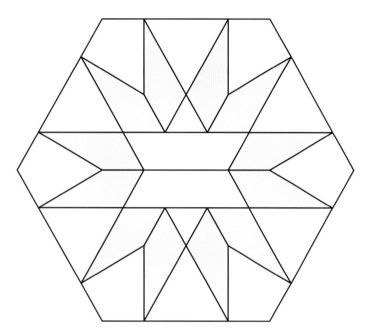

1. Make 6.

2. Join; make 1.

3. Make 2.

4. Make 2.

5. Join; make 2.

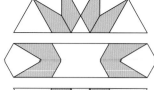

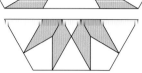

6. Join.

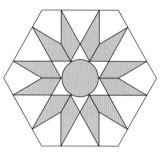

7. Appliqué the circle.

Follow the Leader

TECHNIQUES

Hand piecing, page 10

Center stars, page 14

Adding borders, page 15

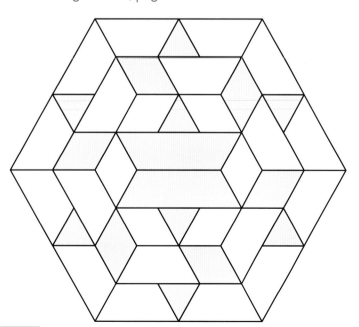

1. Make 1.

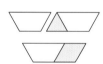

2. Join; make 6.

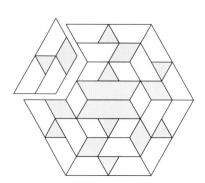

3. Join.

Run Spot Run

TECHNIQUES

Hand piecing, page 10

Appliqué, page 12

Adding borders, page 15

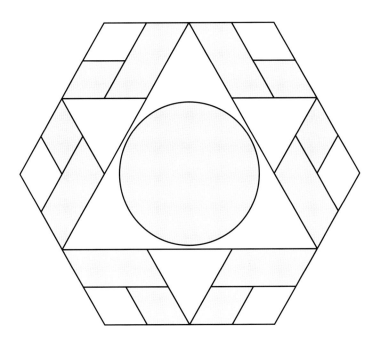

1. Join; make 3.

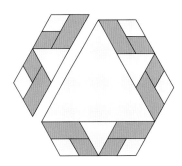

2. Join.

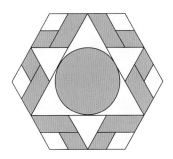

3. Appliqué the circle.

First Bouquet

TECHNIQUES

Hand piecing, page 10

Partial seams, page 13

Adding borders, page 15

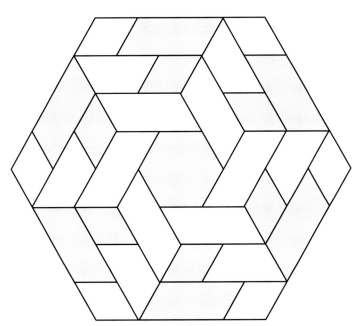

1. Make 6.

2. Join with a partial seam.

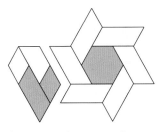

3. Join with a partial seam.

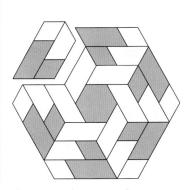

4. Join with a partial seam.

Rosy Cheeks

TECHNIQUES

Hand piecing, page 10

Center stars, page 14

Adding borders, page 15

1. Make 1.

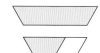

2. Make 6.

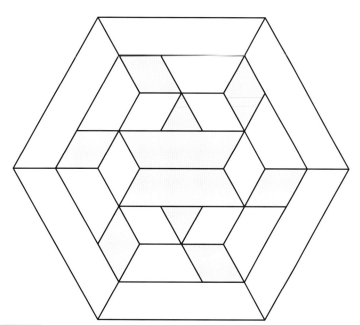

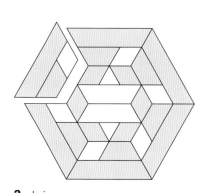

3. Join.

Wallflower Fears

TECHNIQUES

Hand piecing, page 10

Center stars, page 14

Adding borders, page 15

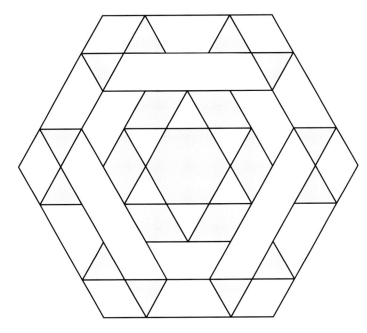

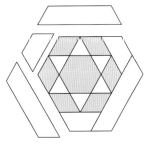

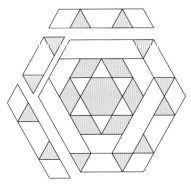

1. Make 1; join.

2. Make 3.

3. Make 3.

4. Join.

Algae Blooms

TECHNIQUES

Hand piecing, page 10

Adding borders, page 15

1. Make 3.

2. Make 3.

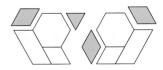

5. Join; make 1.

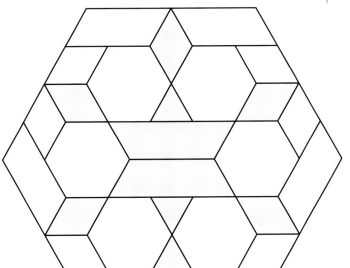

3. Join; make 1.

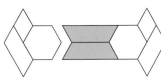

4. Join; make 1.

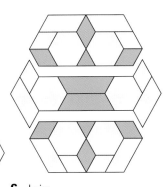

6. Join.

Cat's Eyes

TECHNIQUES

Hand piecing, page 10

Adding borders, page 15

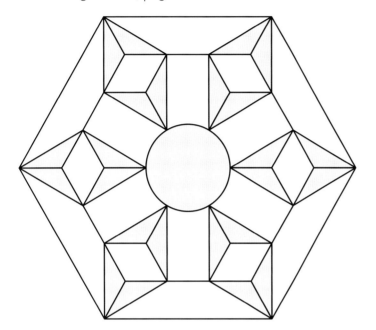

1. Make 6.

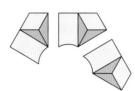

2. Join; make 2.

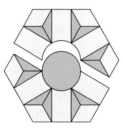

3. Join.

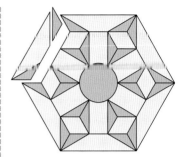

4. Join.

Before the Autumn

TECHNIQUES

Hand piecing, page 10

Adding borders, page 15

1. Make 6.

2. Join; make 1.

3. Make 2.

4. Make 2.

5. Join; make 2.

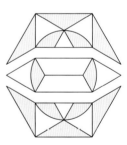

6. Join.

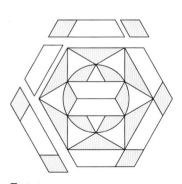

7. Join.

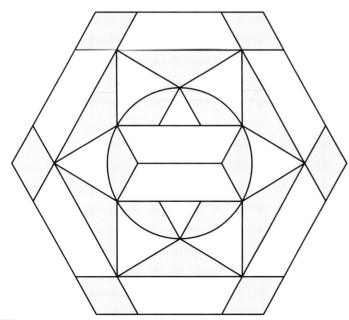

Baby's Bonnet

TECHNIQUES

Hand piecing, page 10

Center stars, page 14

Adding borders, page 15

1. Make 3.

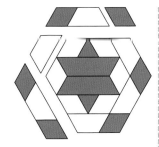

2. Make 1; join.

3. Make 6.

4. Join.

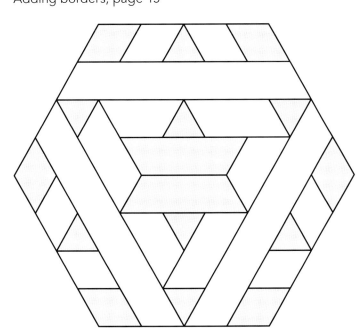

Fields of Heather

TECHNIQUES

Hand piecing, page 10

Center stars, page 14

Adding borders, page 15

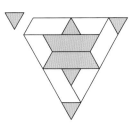

1. Make 1; join.

2. Make 3.

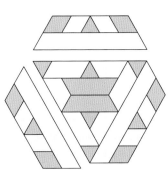

3. Join.

I Remember

TECHNIQUES

Embroidery, page 12

Adding borders, page 15

Threads used: DMC: 815 (Medium Garnet), 355 (Dark Terra Cotta), 356 (Medium Terra Cotta), 754 (Light Peach), 758 (Very Light Terra Cotta), 948 (Very Light Peach), 819 (Light Baby Peach), 819 (Light Baby Pink), 3770 (Very Light Tawny)

Mum

Photo from the White family's collection

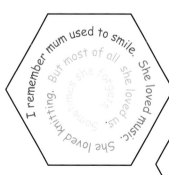

Stitch, using a single thread and changing thread color with every 3 or 4 words.

I remember mum used to smile. But most of all she loved knitting. Sometimes she forgets. She loved music. She loved us.

Winter Grass

TECHNIQUES

Hand piecing, page 10

Adding borders, page 15

1. Make 4.

2. Make 2.

3. Make 2.

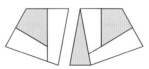

4. Join; make 2.

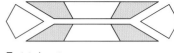

5. Make 1.

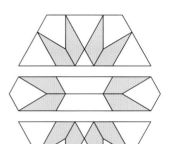

6. Join.

Choices

TECHNIQUES

Hand piecing, page 10

Adding borders, page 15

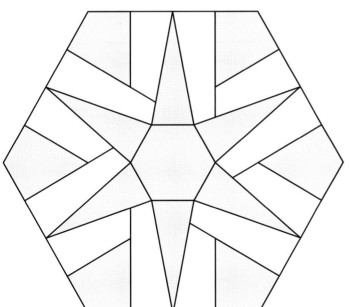

1. Make 6.

2. Join; make 2.

3. Make 2.

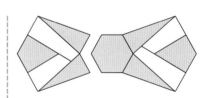

4. Join; make 1.

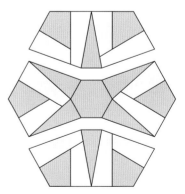

5. Join.

History Repeats

TECHNIQUES

Foundation piecing, page 11

Adding borders, page 15

1. Make 1 of each.

2. Join.

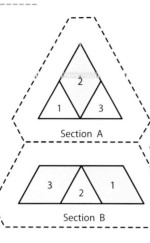

Section A

Section B

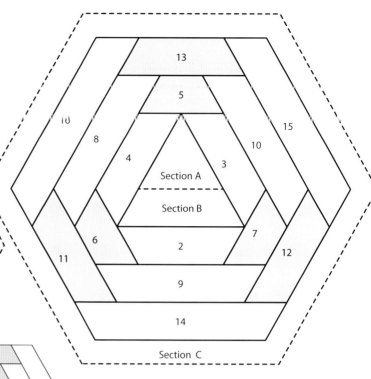

13
5
10
8
15
4
Section A
3
10
Section B
6
2
7
11
9
12
14
Section C

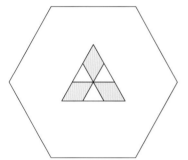

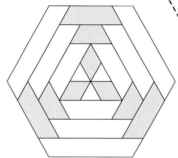

3. Sew AB unit to paper C.

4. Complete C.

Stories Entwined

TECHNIQUES

Hand piecing, page 10

Adding borders, page 15

1. Make 3.

2. Make 3.

3. Join; make 3.

4. Make 3.

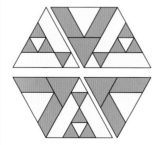

5. Join.

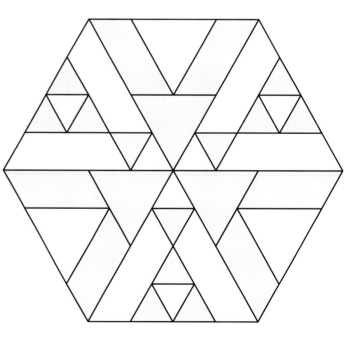

Voices in the Stars

TECHNIQUES

Hand piecing, page 10

Center stars, page 14

Adding borders, page 15

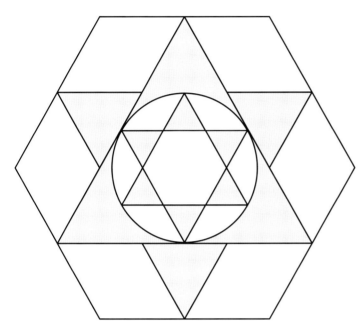

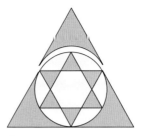

1. Make 1; join.

2. Make 3.

3. Join.

Marmalade

TECHNIQUES

Hand piecing, page 10

Adding borders, page 15

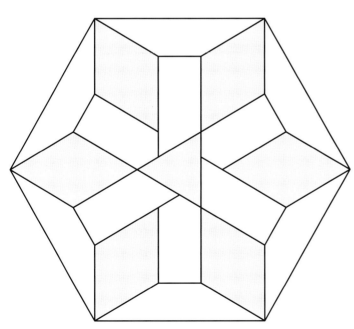

1. Make 3.

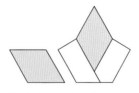

2. Join; make 2.

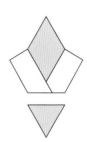

3. Make 1.

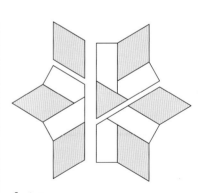

4. Join.

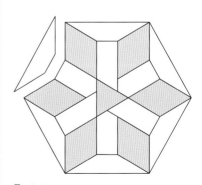

5. Join.

Sugar and Spice

TECHNIQUES

Hand piecing, page 10

Partial seams, page 13

Center stars, page 14

Adding borders, page 15

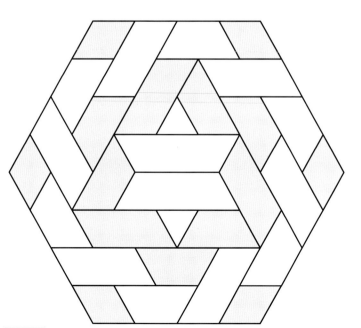

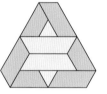

1. Make 1.

2. Make 3.

3. Make 3.

4. Join; make 3.

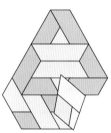

5. Join, using partial seams.

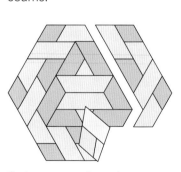

6. Join; complete the partial seams.

Floating Star

TECHNIQUES

Hand piecing, page 10

Adding borders, page 15

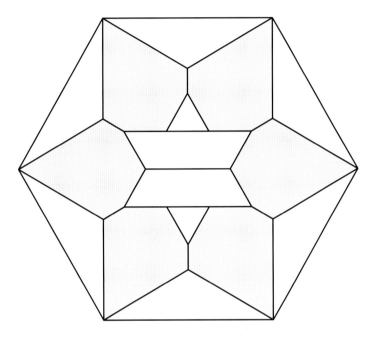

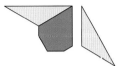

1. Make 2.

2. Join; make 2.

3. Make 1.

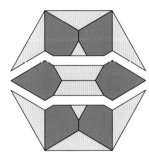

4. Join.

Luca

TECHNIQUES

Hand piecing, page 10

Appliqué, page 12

Adding borders, page 15

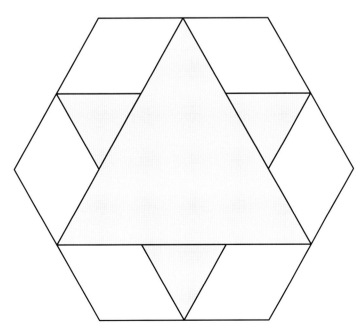

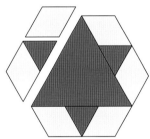

1. Join.

2. Appliqué the dark circle to a light 3″ × 3″ square. Press and trim.

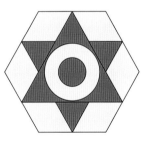

3. Appliqué the circles to the block.

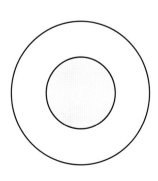

Tinkle of Keys

TECHNIQUES

Hand piecing, page 10

Adding borders, page 15

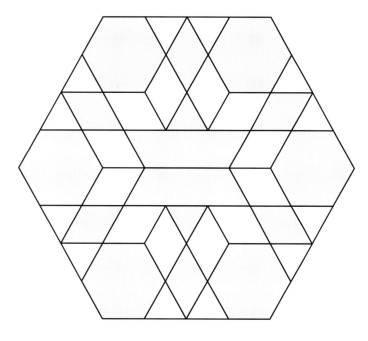

1. Make 4.

2. Make 6.

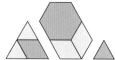

3. Join; make 2.

4. Join; make 2.

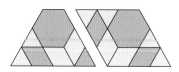

5. Join; make 2.

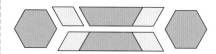

6. Join; make 1.

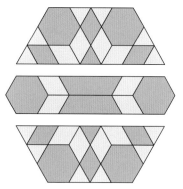

7. Join.

Exploding Star

TECHNIQUES

Hand piecing, page 10

Adding borders, page 15

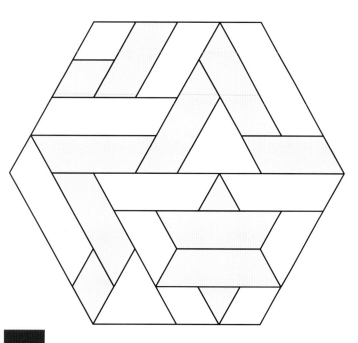

1. Join; make 1.

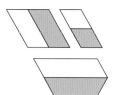

2. Join; make 1.

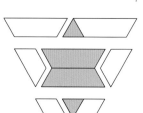

3. Join; make a star.

4. Join; make 1.

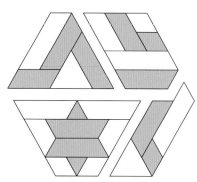

5. Join.

Lady Liberty

TECHNIQUES

Hand piecing, page 10

Adding borders, page 15

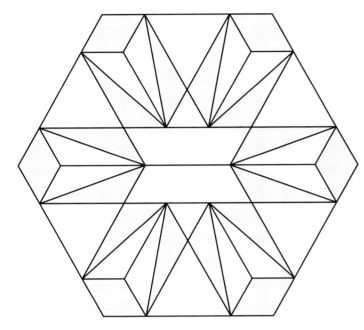

1. Make 4.

2. Make 2.

3. Make 2.

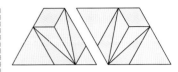

4. Join; make 2.

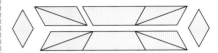

5. Make 1.

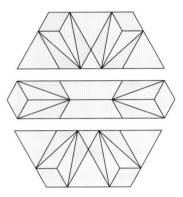

6. Join.

16 Sixth St.

TECHNIQUES

Hand piecing, page 10

Adding borders, page 15

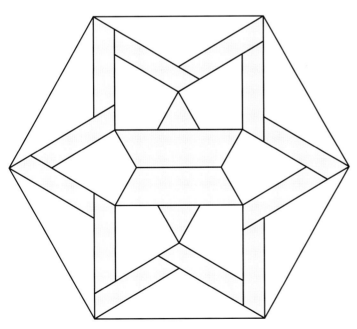

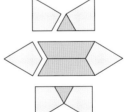

1. Make 1.

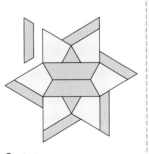

2. Join.

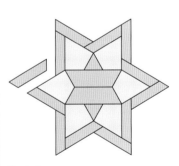

3. Join.

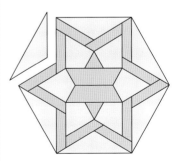

4. Join.

Sunburnt Traditions

TECHNIQUES

Hand piecing, page 10

Adding borders, page 15

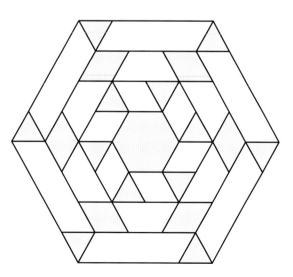

1. Join.

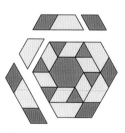

2. Join.

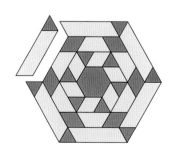

3. Join.

Heart's Desire

TECHNIQUES

Hand piecing, page 10

Partial seams, page 13

Adding borders, page 15

1. Make 6.

2. Make 6.

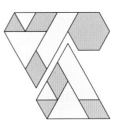

3. Join, using a partial seam.

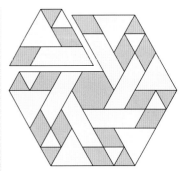

4. Join; complete the partial seam.

Kew Gardens

TECHNIQUES

Hand piecing, page 10

Center stars, page 14

Adding borders, page 15

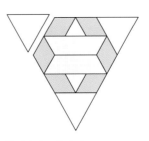

1. Make 1; join.

2. Make 3.

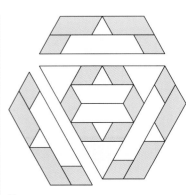

3. Join.

Symmetry in Blue

TECHNIQUES

Hand piecing, page 10

Adding borders, page 15

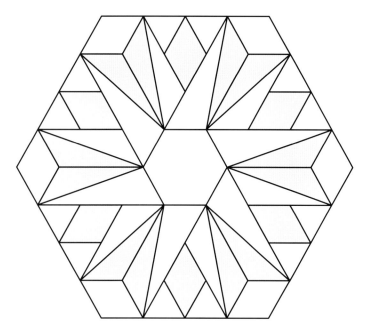

1. Make 6.

2. Make 6.

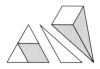

3. Join; make 6.

4. Make 5.

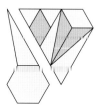

5. Join.

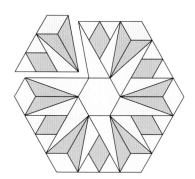

6. Join.

Stilettos

TECHNIQUES

Hand piecing, page 10

Adding borders, page 15

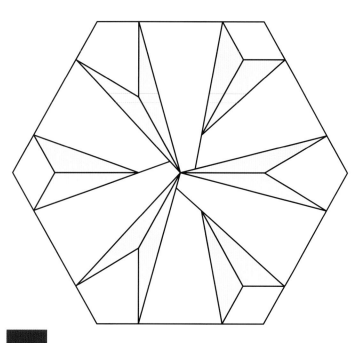

1. Make 3.

2. Join; make 3.

3. Make 3.

4. Join; make 3.

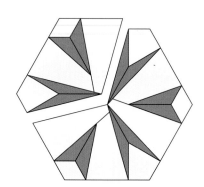

5. Join.

Grandma's Apron

TECHNIQUES

Hand piecing, page 10

Adding borders, page 15

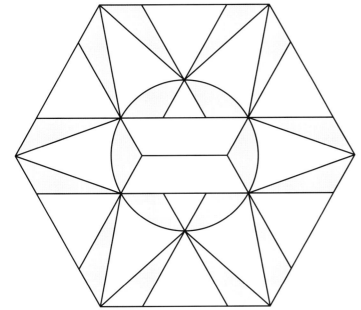

1. Make 6.

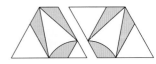

5. Join; make 2.

2. Join; make 1.

3. Make 2.

4. Make 2.

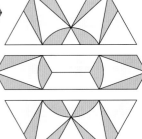

6. Join.

North for the Winter

TECHNIQUES

Hand piecing, page 10

Adding borders, page 15

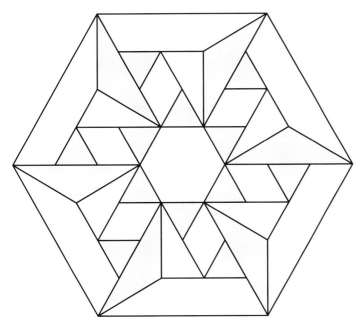

1. Make 6.

2. Join; make 6.

3. Join; make 6.

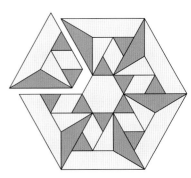

4. Join.

Images of Claire

TECHNIQUES

Foundation piecing, page 11

Adding borders, page 15

1. Make 1 of each.

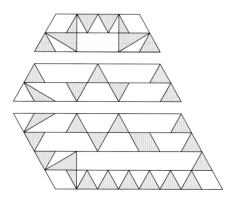

2. Join.

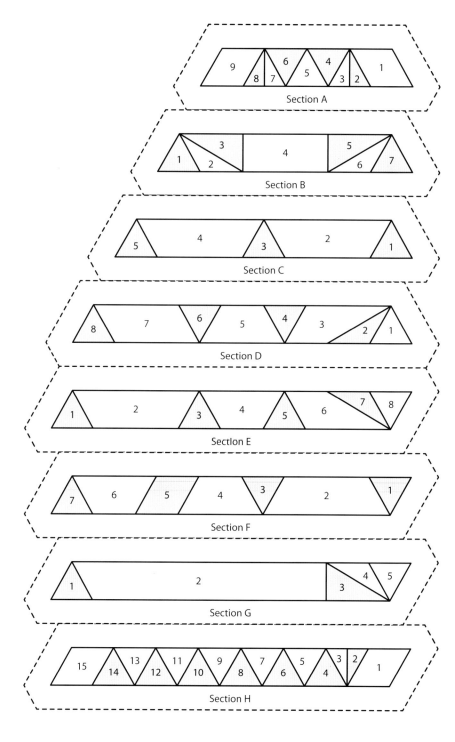

Poison Woman

TECHNIQUES

Foundation piecing, page 11

Adding borders, page 15

1. Make 1 of each.

2. Join.

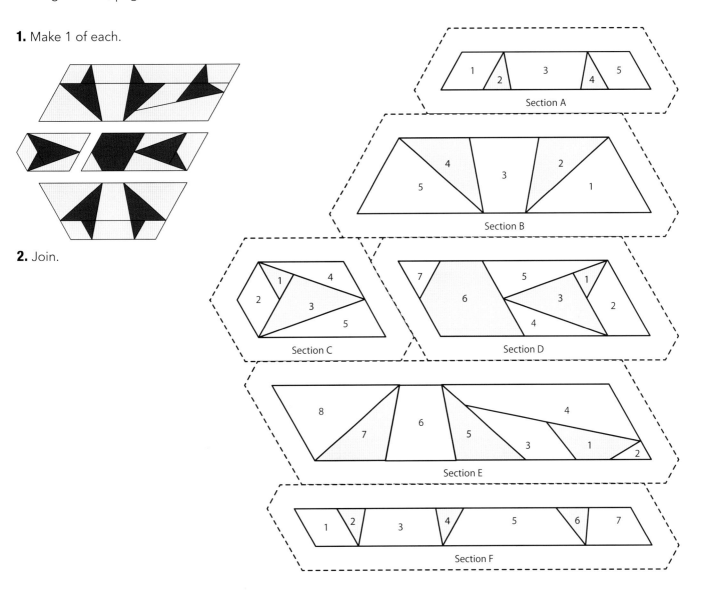

Section A

Section B

Section C

Section D

Section E

Section F

English Garden

TECHNIQUES

Hand piecing, page 10

Adding borders, page 15

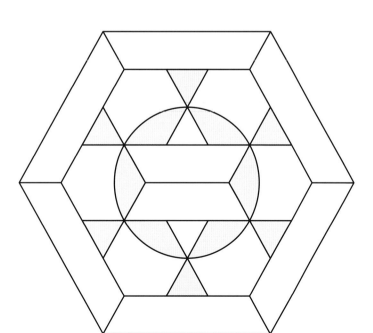

1. Make 1.

2. Make 2.

3. Make 2.

4. Join; make 2.

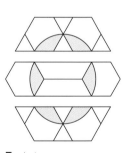

5. Join.

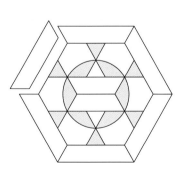

6. Join.

White Wall Tiles

TECHNIQUES

Hand piecing, page 10

Adding borders, page 15

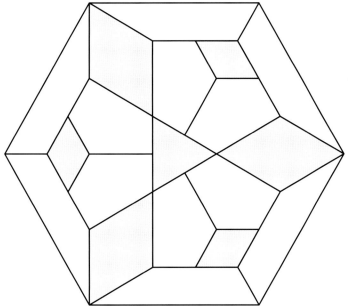

1. Make 3.

2. Make 2.

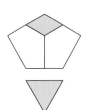

3. Make 1.

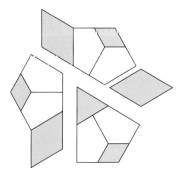

4. Join.

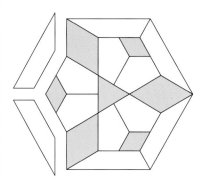

5. Join.

Follow Your Heart

TECHNIQUES

Appliqué, page 12

Adding borders, page 15

Appliqué, using your preferred method.

Blue Moon

TECHNIQUES

Hand piecing, page 10

Appliqué, page 13

Adding borders, page 15

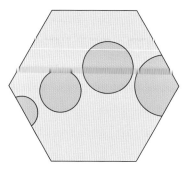

Appliqué, using your preferred method.

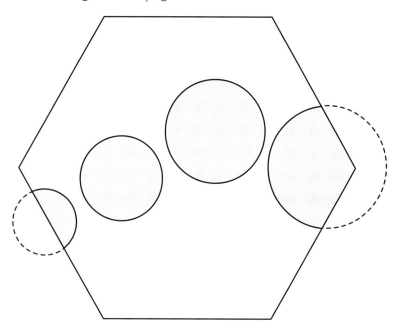

Through the Roses

TECHNIQUES

Foundation piecing, page 11

Adding borders, page 15

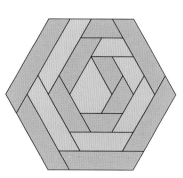

Make 1.

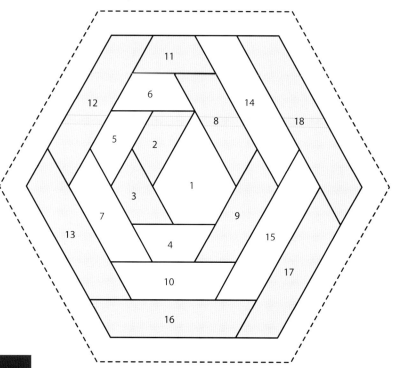

Solid Gold

TECHNIQUES

Hand piecing, page 10

Center stars, page 14

Adding borders, page 15

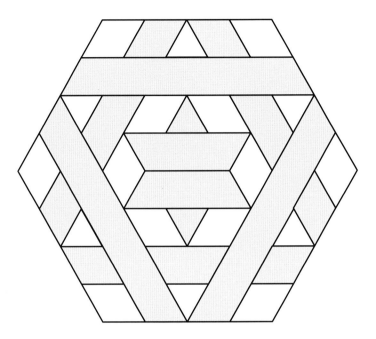

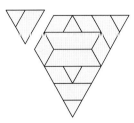

1. Make 1; join.

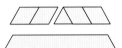

2. Make 3.

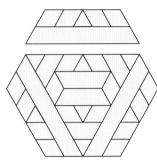

3. Join.

Champs-Élysées Alight

TECHNIQUES

Hand piecing, page 10

Center stars, page 14

Adding borders, page 15

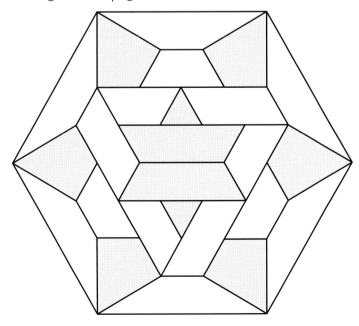

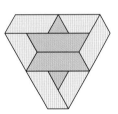

1. Make 1.

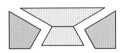

2. Make 3.

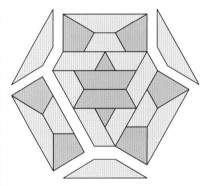

3. Join.

Raconteur

TECHNIQUES

Embroidery, page 12

Adding borders, page 15

Raconteur

The Storyteller's Collection

Cinzia White

2007 - 2012

Stitch, using a single
strand of DMC 355
(Dark Terra Cotta).

Raconteur

The Storyteller's Collection

Cinzia White

2007 - 2012

Reflections

TECHNIQUES

Foundation piecing, page 11

Adding borders, page 15

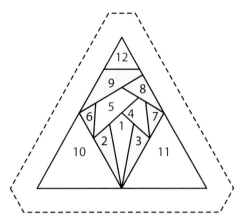

1. Make 6.

2. Join.

Bamboozled

TECHNIQUES

Foundation piecing, page 11

Adding borders, page 15

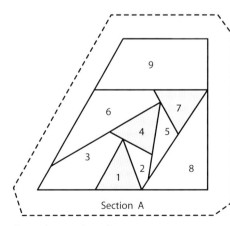

Section A

Section B

1. Make 2 of each.

2. Join.

Stringing Away

TECHNIQUES

Foundation piecing, page 11

Adding borders, page 15

1. Make 1 of each.

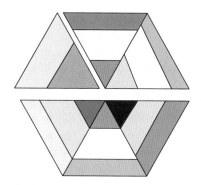

2. Join.

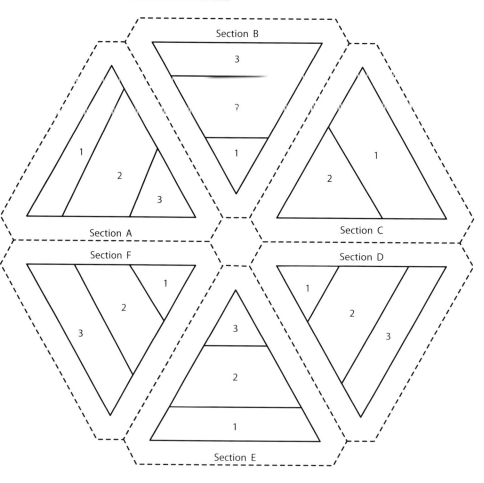

Section B

Section A

Section C

Section F

Section D

Section E

Reunion

TECHNIQUES

Hand piecing, page 10

Adding borders, page 15

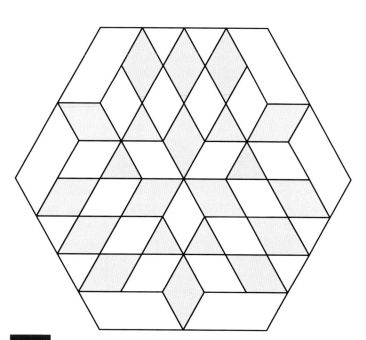

1. Make 3.

2. Make 3.

3. Join.

4. Join.

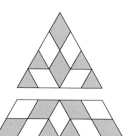

5. Join.

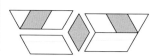

6. Make 3.

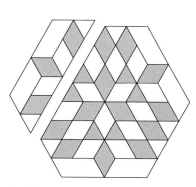

7. Join.

Winter Blossoms

TECHNIQUES

Hand piecing, page 10

Adding borders, page 15

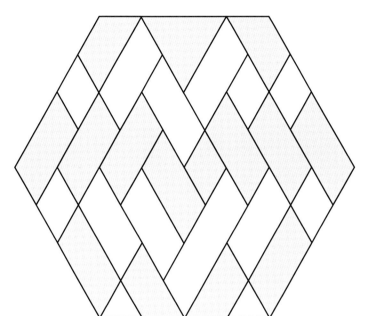

1. Make 1.

2. Join; make 1.

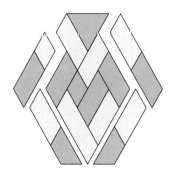

3. Join; make 1.

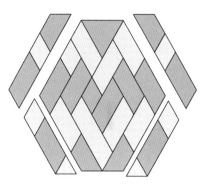

4. Join.

No Way Out

TECHNIQUES

Hand piecing, page 10

Adding borders, page 15

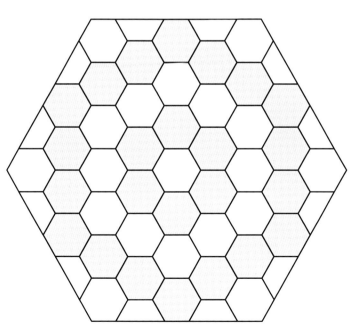

1. Make 1.

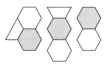

2. Make 6.

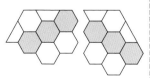

3. Join; make 2.

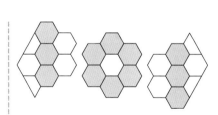

4. Join; make 1.

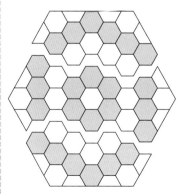

5. Join.

Starburst

TECHNIQUES

Hand piecing, page 10

Adding borders, page 15

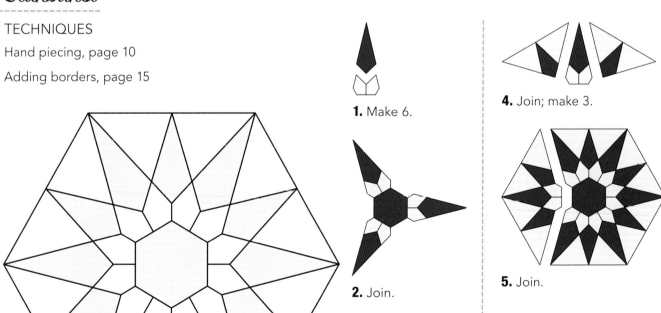

1. Make 6.

2. Join.

3. Make 6.

4. Join; make 3.

5. Join.

Nine to Five

TECHNIQUES

Hand piecing, page 10

Adding borders, page 15

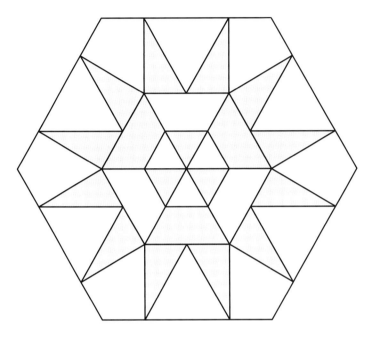

1. Make 6.

2. Make 3.

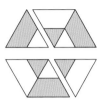

3. Join.

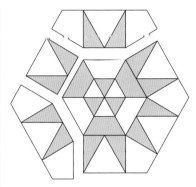

4. Join.

Eye of the Storm

TECHNIQUES

Hand piecing, page 10

Center stars, page 14

Adding borders, page 15

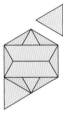

1. Make 1; join.

2. Make 6.

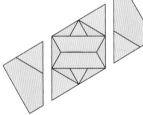

3. Join; make 1.

4. Make 2.

5. Make 2.

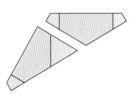

6. Join; make 2.

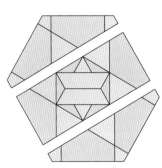

7. Join.

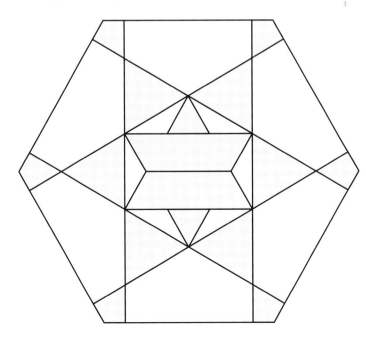

Raspberry Ripple

TECHNIQUES

Foundation piecing, page 11

Adding borders, page 15

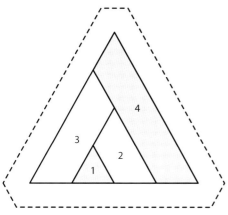

1. Make 6.

2. Join.

The Dish

TECHNIQUES

Hand piecing, page 10

Adding borders, page 15

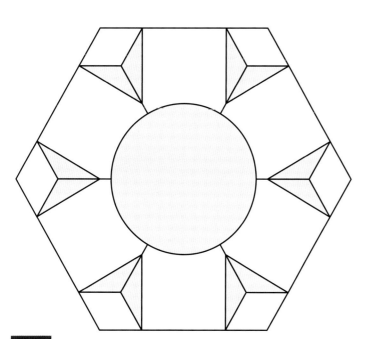

1. Make 6.

2. Make 6.

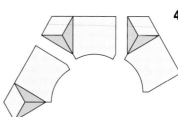

3. Join; make 2.

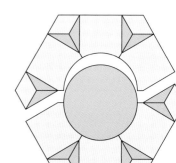

4. Join.

Twirl with Me

TECHNIQUES

Hand piecing, page 10

Adding borders, page 15

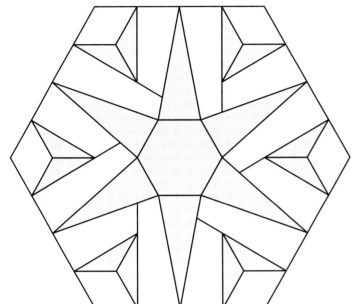

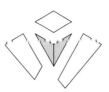

1. Make 6.

2. Join; make 2.

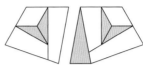

3. Make 2.

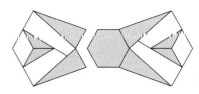

4. Join; make 1.

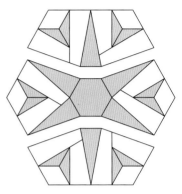

5. Join.

Blue Diamond

TECHNIQUES

Hand piecing, page 10

Adding borders, page 15

1. Make 6.

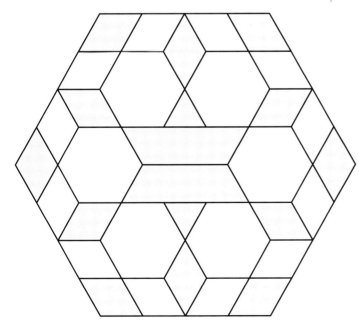

2. Join; make 1.

3. Make 2.

4. Make 2.

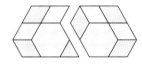

5. Join; make 2.

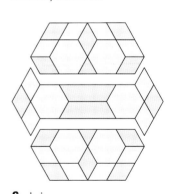

6. Join.

Fish Kiss

TECHNIQUES

Hand piecing, page 10

Adding borders, page 15

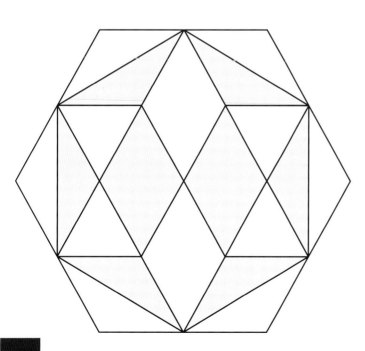

1. Make 4.

2. Make 1.

3. Join; make 1.

4. Make 2.

5. Join.

Stolen Threads

TECHNIQUES

Hand piecing, page 10

Center stars, page 14

Adding borders, page 15

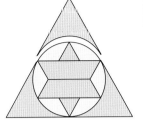

1. Make 1.

2. Make 3.

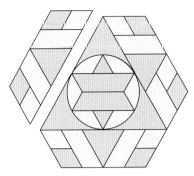

3. Join.

Temple Within

TECHNIQUES

Hand piecing, page 10

Adding borders, page 15

1. Make 1.

2. Join.

3. Join.

4. Make 1.

5. Make 1.

6. Join.

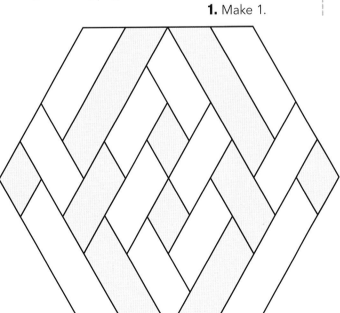

Summer Sun

TECHNIQUES

Hand piecing, page 10

Adding borders, page 15

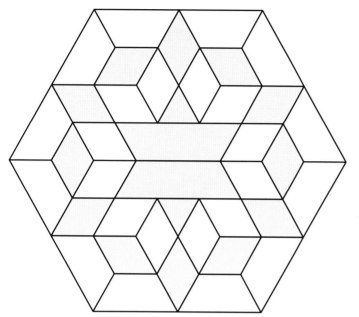

1. Make 6.

2. Join; make 1.

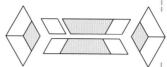

3. Make 2.

4. Make 2.

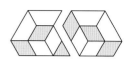

5. Join; make 2.

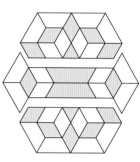

6. Join.

Alexander's Gold

TECHNIQUES

Hand piecing, page 10

Center stars, page 14

Adding borders, page 15

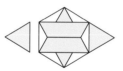

1. Make 1; join.

2. Make 6.

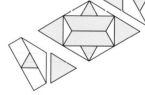

3. Join; make 1.

4. Make 2.

5. Make 2.

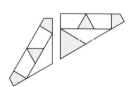

6. Join; make 2.

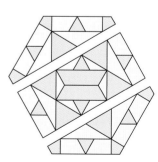

7. Join.

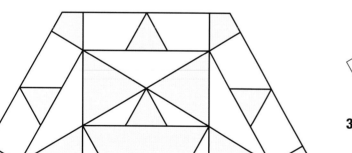

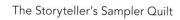

Bounds of Hope

TECHNIQUES

Hand piecing, page 10

Center stars, page 14

Adding borders, page 15

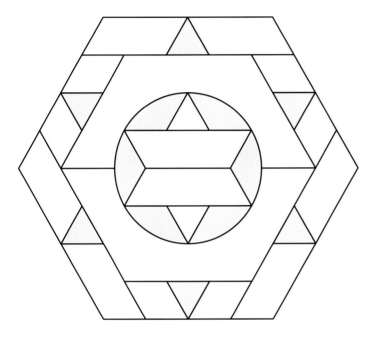

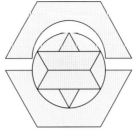

1. Join; make 1.

2. Join; make 3.

3. Make 3.

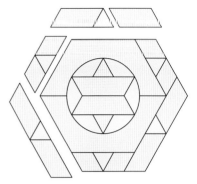

4. Join.

Twisting Maze

TECHNIQUES

Hand piecing, page 10

Adding borders, page 15

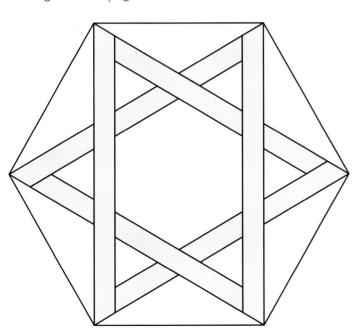

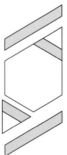

1. Join, make 1.

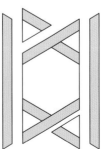

2. Join; make 1.

3. Join; make 1.

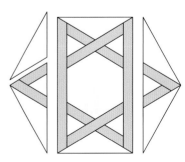

4. Join.

Hearts Abound

TECHNIQUES

Hand piecing, page 10

Partial seams, page 13

Adding borders, page 15

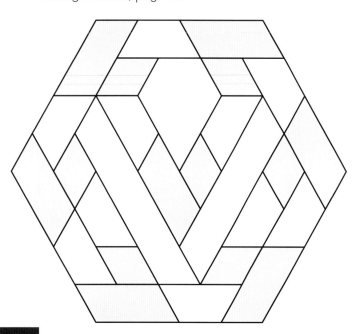

1. Make 1.

2. Make 1.

3. Make 2.

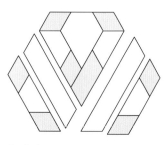

4. Join.

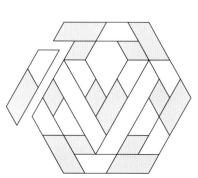

5. Join with partial seams.

Splendor of the Storm

TECHNIQUES

Hand piecing, page 10

Adding borders, page 15

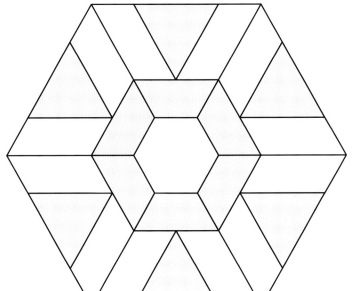

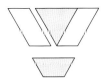

1. Make 6.

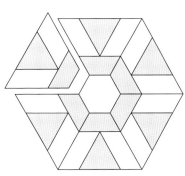

2. Join.

Chinese Checkers

TECHNIQUES

Foundation piecing, page 11

Adding borders, page 15

1. Make 1 of each.

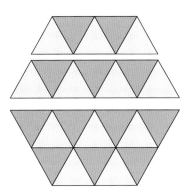

2. Join.

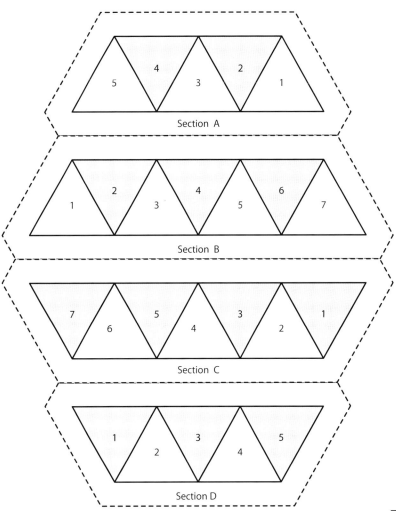

Strawberry Shortcake

TECHNIQUES

Hand piecing, page 10

Adding borders, page 15

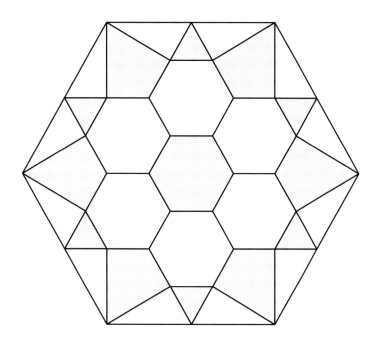

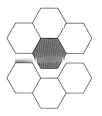

1. Make 1.

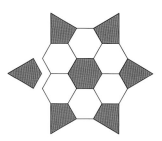

2. Join.

3. Make 6.

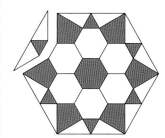

4. Join.

Round and Round

TECHNIQUES

Hand piecing, page 10

Adding borders, page 15

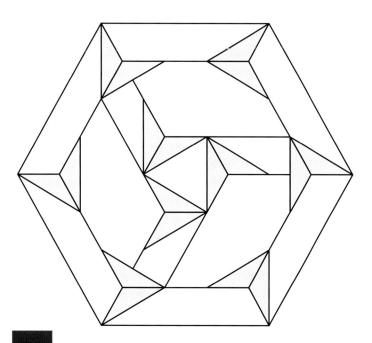

1. Make 3.

2. Join.

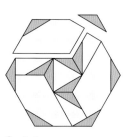

3. Join.

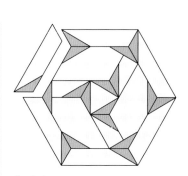

4. Join.

COLLECTION 38

Coeur d'Or

TECHNIQUES

Hand piecing, page 10

Adding borders, page 15

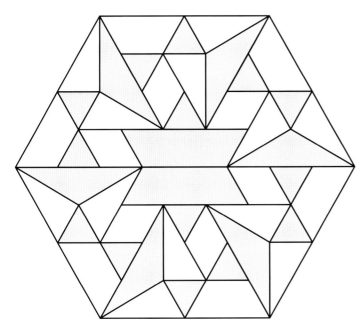

1. Make 2.

2. Make 4.

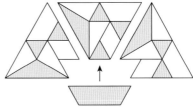

3. Join; make 2.

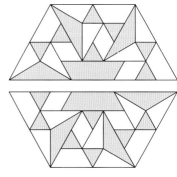

4. Join.

Tempest

TECHNIQUES

Hand piecing, page 10

Adding borders, page 15

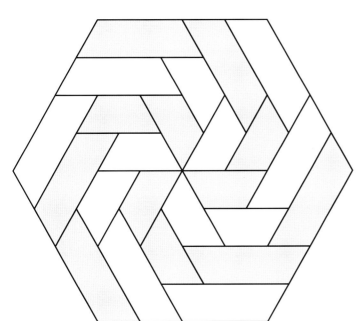

1. Make 1.

2. Join.

3. Join.

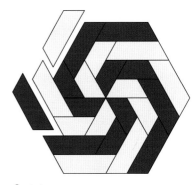

4. Join.

Cotton Candy

TECHNIQUES
Hand piecing, page 10

Adding borders, page 15

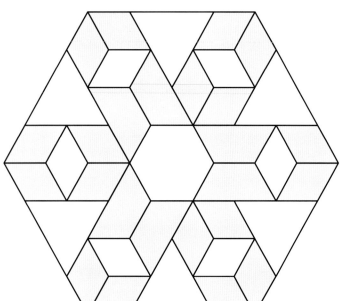

1. Make 3.

2. Join.

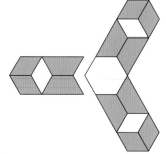

3. Make 3.

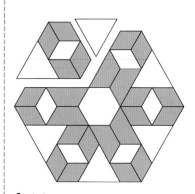

4. Join.

Tutu in the Snow

TECHNIQUES

Hand piecing, page 10

Adding borders, page 15

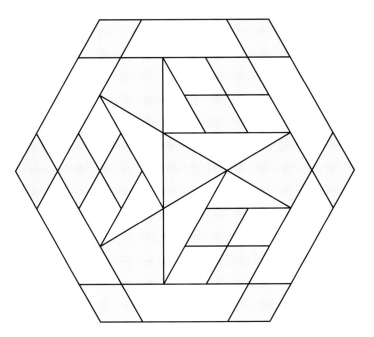

1. Make 3.

2. Make 3.

3. Make 2.

4. Make 1.

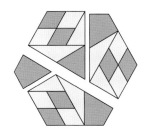

5. Join.

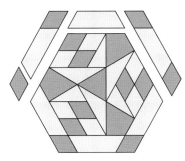

6. Join.

Ripples

TECHNIQUES

Hand piecing, page 10

Center stars, page 14

Adding borders, page 15

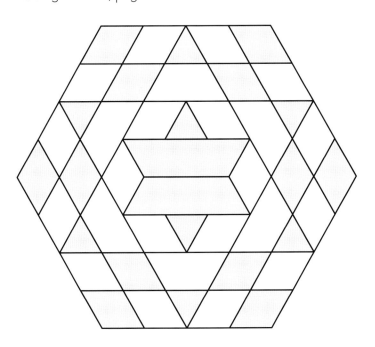

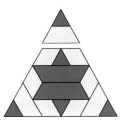

1. Make 1; join.

2. Make 6.

3. Join; make 3.

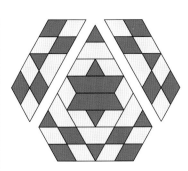

4. Join.

Mums for Mum

TECHNIQUES

Hand piecing, page 10

Center stars, page 14

Adding borders, page 15

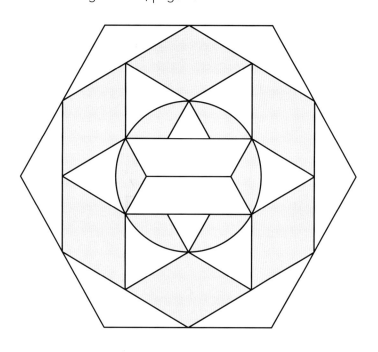

1. Make 2.

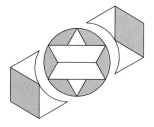

2. Make 1; join.

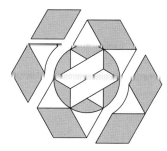

3. Join.

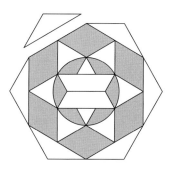

4. Join.

Fluorescent Moss

TECHNIQUES

Hand piecing, page 10

Adding borders, page 15

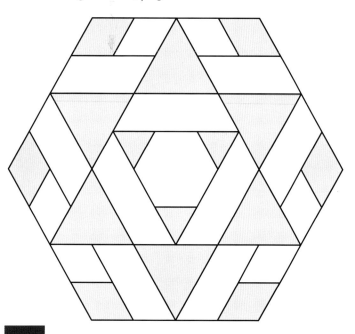

1. Make 1.

2. Make 3.

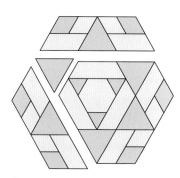

3. Join.

New Grid

TECHNIQUES

Hand piecing, page 10

Partial seams, page 13

Adding borders, page 15

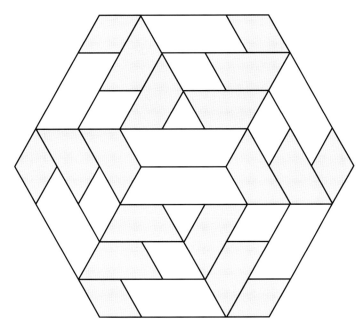

1. Make 6.

2. Join; make 2.

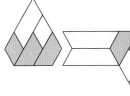

3. Join with partial seams.

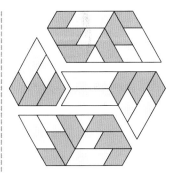

4. Join; complete the partial seams.

Monkey in the Middle

TECHNIQUES

Hand piecing, page 10

Center stars, page 14

Adding borders, page 15

1. Make 3.

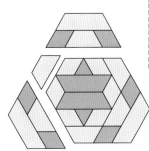

2. Make 1; join.

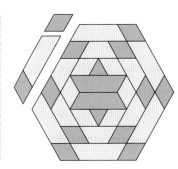

3. Join.

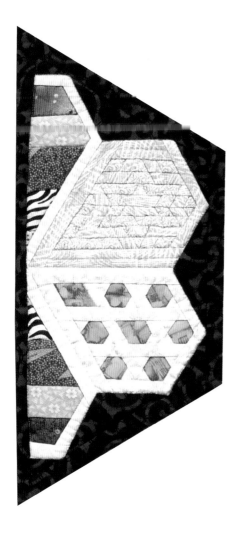

The Star Within

TECHNIQUES

Foundation piecing, page 11

Adding borders, page 15

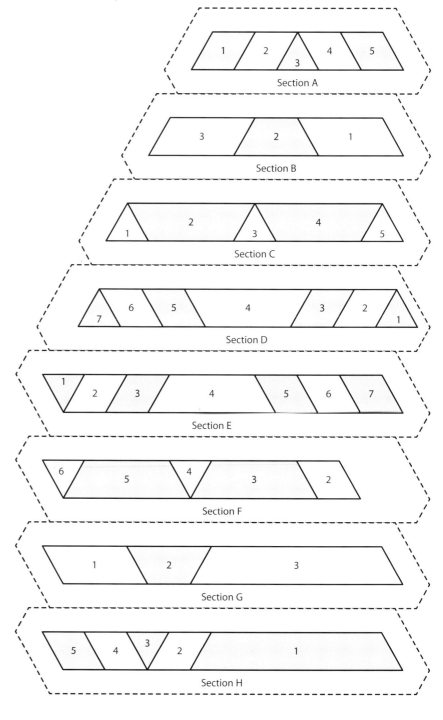

Section A

Section B

Section C

Section D

Section E

Section F

Section G

Section H

1. Make 1 of each.

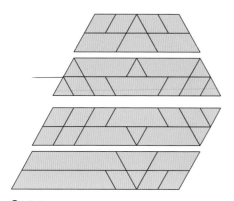

2. Join.

Tangled Web

TECHNIQUES

Hand piecing, page 10

Adding borders, page 15

1. Make 1.

2. Make 1.

3. Make 4.

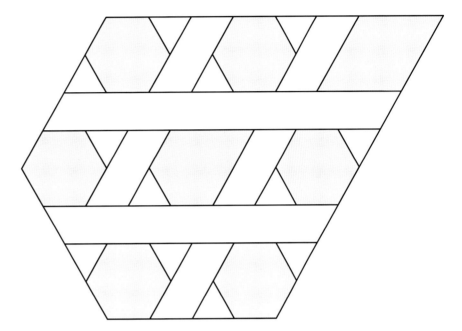

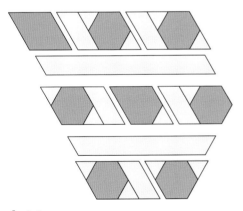

4. Join.

Windmills from the Fair

TECHNIQUES

Hand piecing, page 10

Adding borders, page 15

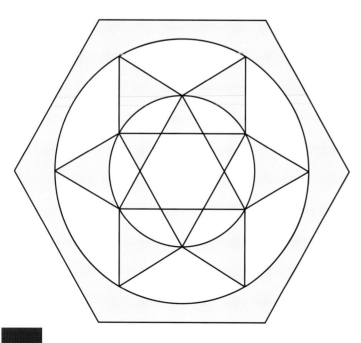

1. Make 4.

2. Join; make 1.

3. Join; make 2.

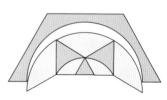

4. Join.

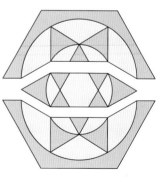

5. Join.

Twisted Bunting

TECHNIQUES

Hand piecing, page 10

Adding borders, page 15

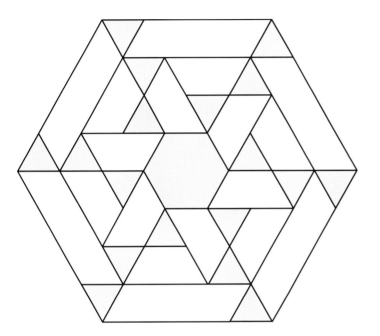

1. Make 6.

2. Make 6.

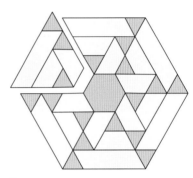

3. Join.

Clean Solutions

TECHNIQUES

Hand piecing, page 10

Adding borders, page 15

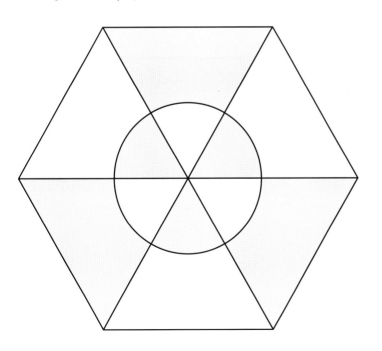

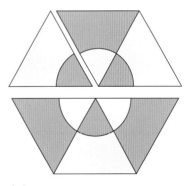

Join.

Let Me Fly

TECHNIQUES

Hand piecing, page 10

Adding borders, page 15

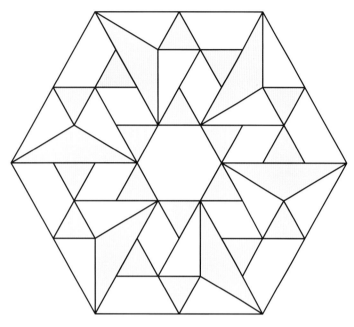

1. Make 6.

2. Make 6.

3. Join; make 6.

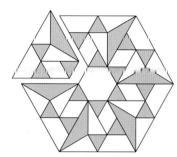

4. Join.

Summer Frock

TECHNIQUES

Hand piecing, page 10

Adding borders, page 15

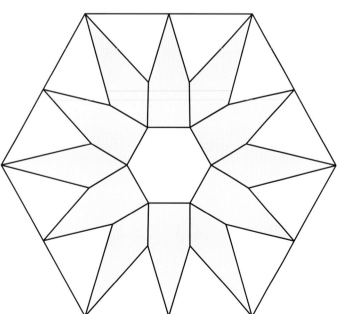

1. Make 6.

2. Join; make 2.

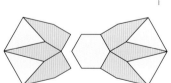

3. Make 1.

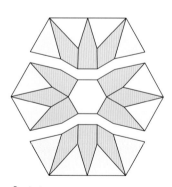

4. Join.

Mud Pies

TECHNIQUES

Hand piecing, page 10

Partial seams, page 13

Adding borders, page 15

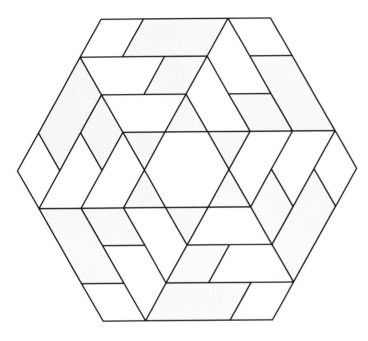

1. Make 6.

2. Make 4.

3. Join, make 2.

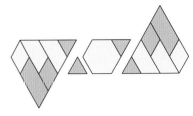

4. Join with partial seams.

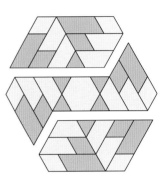

5. Join; complete the partial seams.

Halloween

TECHNIQUES

Hand piecing, page 10

Adding borders, page 15

1. Make 3.

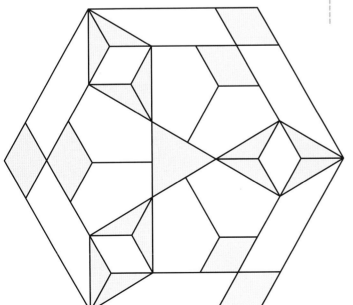

2. Make 3.

3. Join; make 2.

4. Make 1.

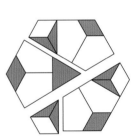

5. Join.

6. Make 3.

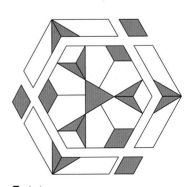

7. Join.

Ruby Red

TECHNIQUES

Hand piecing, page 10

Adding borders, page 15

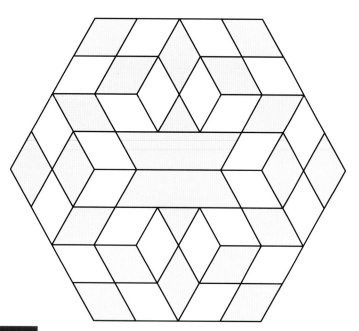

1. Make 2.

2. Make 6.

3. Make 2.

4. Make 1.

5. Join.

The Two of Us

TECHNIQUES

Hand piecing, page 10

Adding borders, page 15

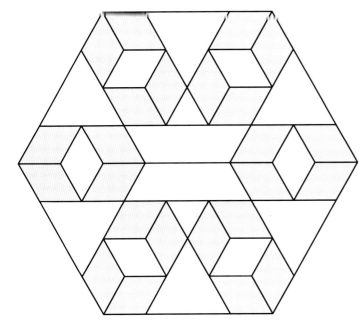

1. Make 6.

2. Join; make 1.

3. Make 2.

4. Make 2.

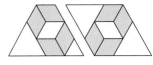

5. Join; make 2.

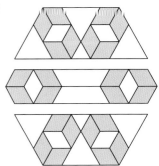

6. Join.

Bouquet for Mary

TECHNIQUES

Hand piecing, page 10

Adding borders, page 15

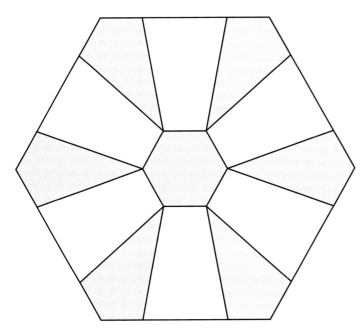

1. Make 2.

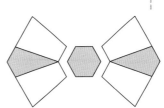

2. Join; make 1.

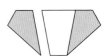

3. Make 2.

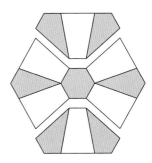

4. Join.

Reaching Out

TECHNIQUES

Hand piecing, page 10

Adding borders, page 15

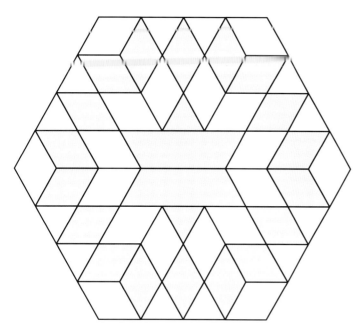

1. Make 4.

2. Make 6.

3. Make 2.

4. Make 2.

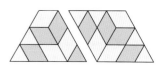

5. Join; make 2.

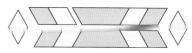

6. Make 1.

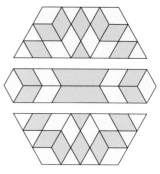

7. Join.

Within

TECHNIQUES

Hand piecing, page 10

Center stars, page 14

Adding borders, page 15

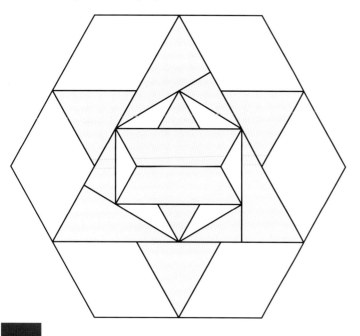

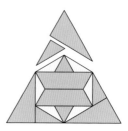

1. Make 1; join.

2. Make 3.

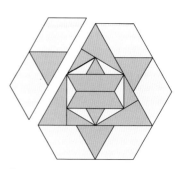

3. Join.

Twirling Dervish

TECHNIQUES

Hand piecing, page 10

Adding borders, page 15

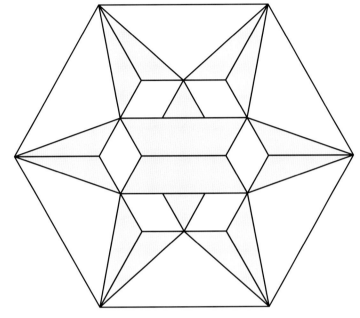

1. Make 6.

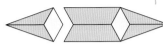

2. Join; make 1.

3. Make 2.

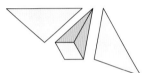

4. Make 2.

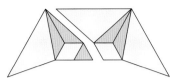

5. Join; make 2.

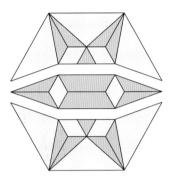

6. Join.

Christabella

TECHNIQUES

Hand piecing, page 10

Adding borders, page 15

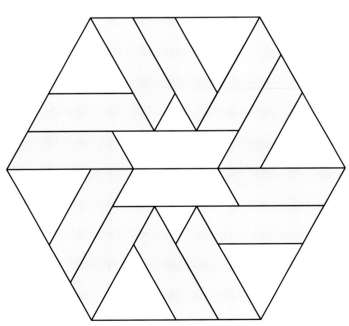

1. Make 6.

2. Join; make 2.

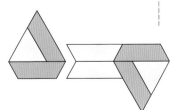

3. Make 1.

4. Join.

Bottled Lemons

TECHNIQUES

Hand piecing, page 10

Adding borders, page 15

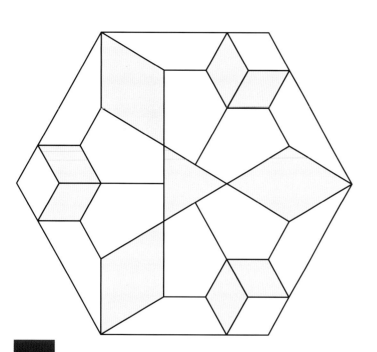

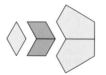

1. Make 3.

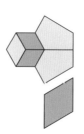

2. Make 2.

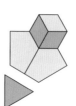

3. Make 1.

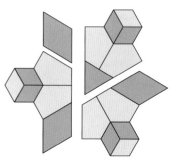

4. Join.

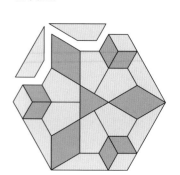

5. Join.

Flying Free

TECHNIQUES

Hand piecing, page 10

Adding borders, page 15

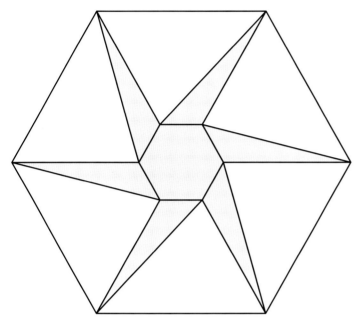

1. Make 6.

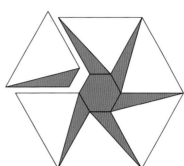

2. Join.

Ebony in Roses

TECHNIQUES

Hand piecing, page 10

Center stars, page 14

Adding borders, page 15

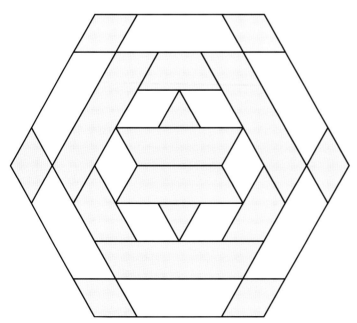

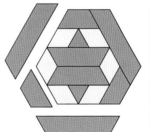

1. Make 1; join.

2. Make 3.

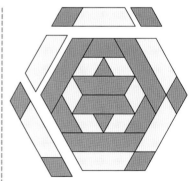

3. Join.

Love Is Blind

TECHNIQUES

Hand piecing, page 10

Partial seams, page 13

Center stars, page 14

Adding borders, page 15

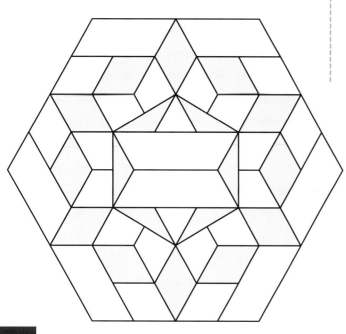

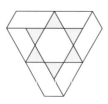

1. Make 1.

2. Make 3.

3. Make 3.

4. Join; make 3.

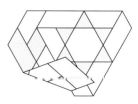

5. Join, using a partial seam.

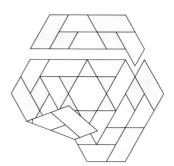

6. Join; complete the partial seam.

Round Two

TECHNIQUES

Hand piecing, page 10

Center stars, page 14

Adding borders, page 15

1. Make 3.

2. Join; make 2.

3. Make 3.

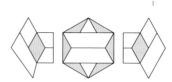

4. Make a star; join.

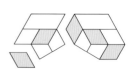

5. Join; make 1.

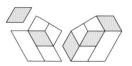

6. Join; make 1.

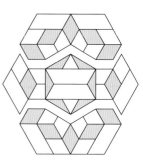

7. Join.

Level One

TECHNIQUES

Hand piecing, page 10

Adding borders, page 15

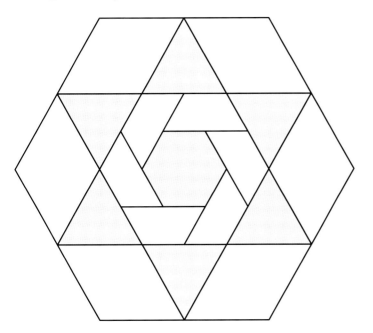

1. Join.

2. Make 3.

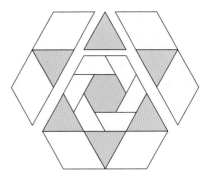

3. Join.

Just There

TECHNIQUES

Hand piecing, page 10

Adding borders, page 15

1. Make 6.

2. Make 2.

4. Join; make 2.

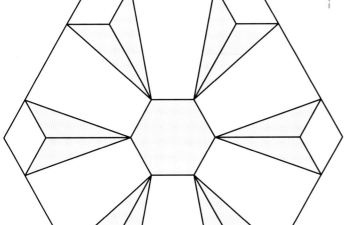

3. Join; make 1.

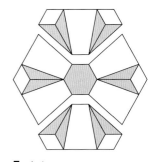

5. Join.

Winter Secrets Too

TECHNIQUES

Embroidery, page 12

Adding borders, page 15

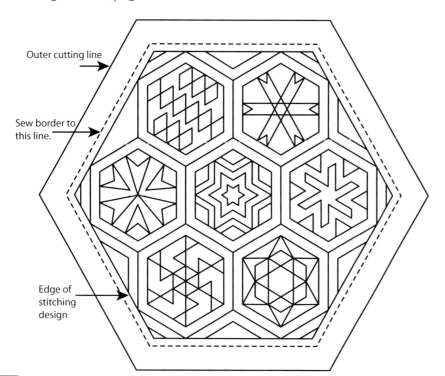

Outer cutting line

Sew border to
this line.

Edge of
stitching
design

1. Stitch, using a single thread.

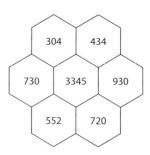

304	434	
730	3345	930
552	720	

2. DMC thread colors;
use DMC 3853 (Dark
Autumn Gold / orange)
for the outlines.

Ant's Trail

TECHNIQUES

Hand piecing, page 10

Foundation piecing, page 11

Trimming oversize blocks, page 13

Partial seams, page 13

Adding borders, page 15

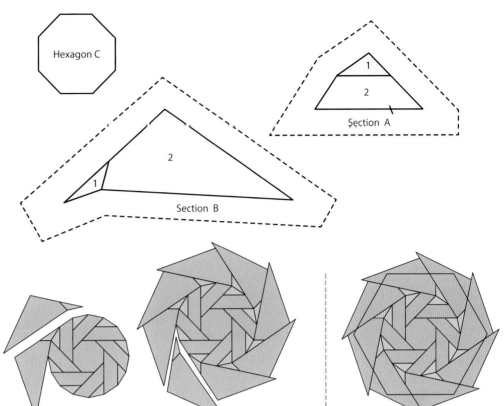

1. Make 8 of each.

2. With hand stitching, join A to C with a partial seam.

3. With hand stitching, join B to AC. Complete the partial seam.

4. Press and trim the block.

The Emperor's Hat

TECHNIQUES

Hand piecing, page 10

Adding borders, page 15

1. Make 2.

2. Make 2.

3. Join; make 2.

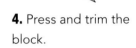

4. Make 1.

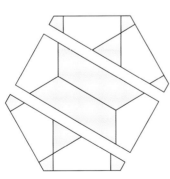

5. Join.

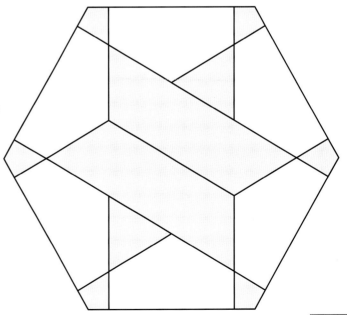

Stripes Rule

TECHNIQUES

Foundation piecing, page 11

Adding borders, page 15

Note: Take care with the direction of the stripes.

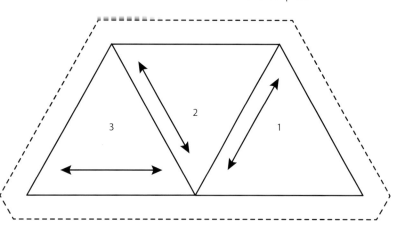

1. Make 2.

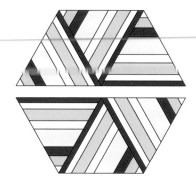

2. Join.

First Flower

TECHNIQUES

Hand piecing, page 10

Adding borders, page 15

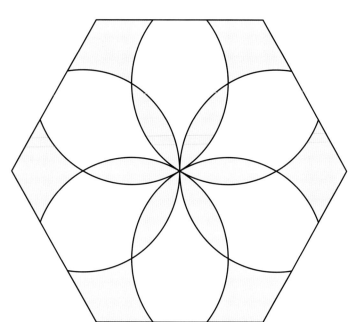

1. Make 3.

2. Join; make 1.

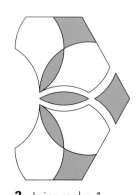

3. Join; make 1.

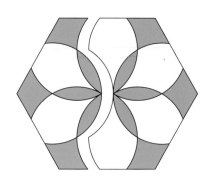

4. Join.

Khanam's Gift

TECHNIQUES

Hand piecing, page 10

Adding borders, page 15

1. Make 1.

2. Join; make 1.

3. Make 1.

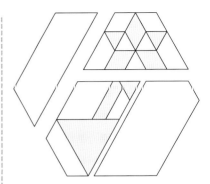

4. Join.

Morning After

TECHNIQUES

Hand piecing, page 10

Adding borders, page 15

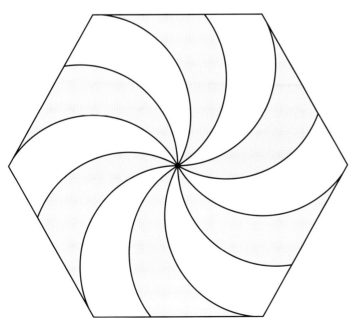

1. Make 2.

2. Make 2.

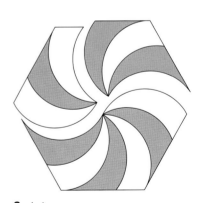

3. Join.

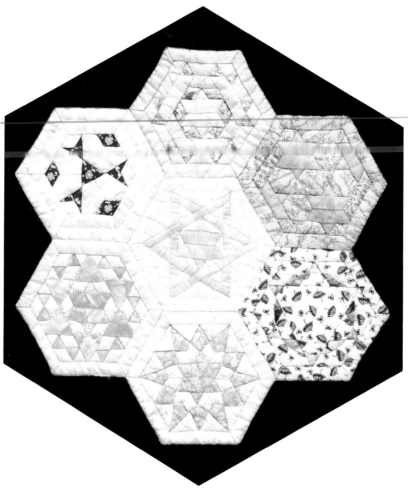

Fizzle

TECHNIQUES

Hand piecing, page 10

Center stars, page 14

Adding borders, page 15

1. Make 1.

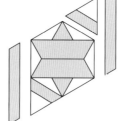

2. Join.

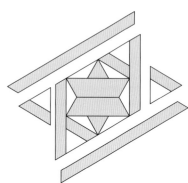

3. Join.

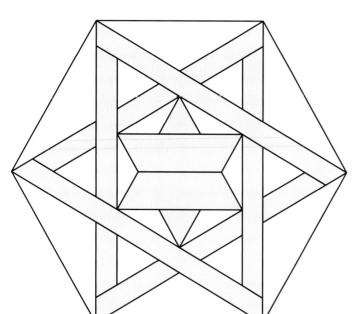

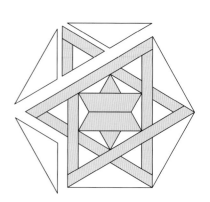

4. Join.

Grandma Wore Blue

TECHNIQUES

Hand piecing, page 10

Center stars, page 14

Adding borders, page 15

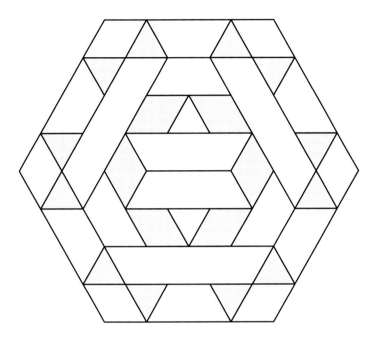

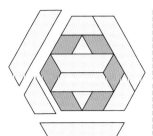

1. Make 1; join.

2. Make 3.

3. Make 3.

4. Join.

Lights of Diwali

TECHNIQUES

Hand piecing, page 10

Adding borders, page 15

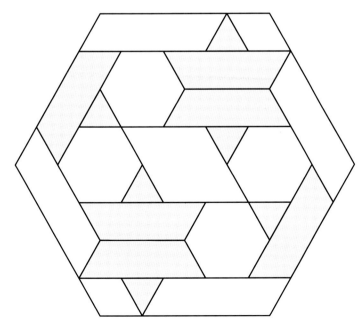

1. Make 2.

2. Make 1.

3. Join; make 1.

4. Join; make 2.

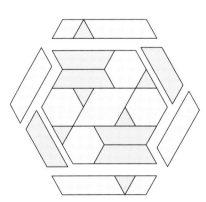

5. Join.

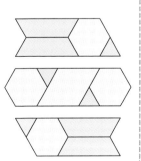

April Showers

TECHNIQUES

Hand piecing, page 10

Adding borders, page 15

1. Make 3.

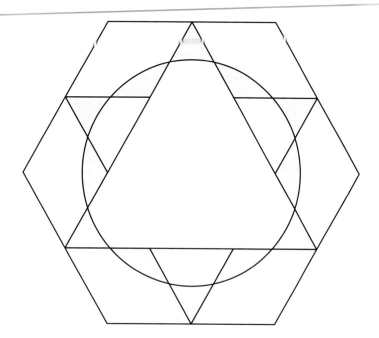

2. Join.

February

TECHNIQUES

Hand piecing, page 10

Adding borders, page 15

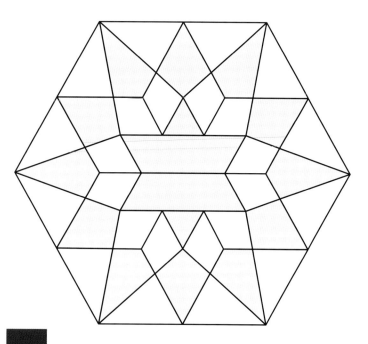

1. Make 6.

2. Make 4.

3. Join; make 2.

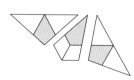

4. Join; make 2.

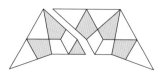

5. Join; make 2.

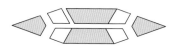

6. Make 1.

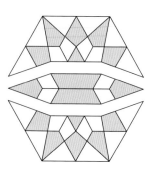

7. Join.

Dancing Flames

TECHNIQUES

Hand piecing, page 10

Center stars, page 14

Adding borders, page 15

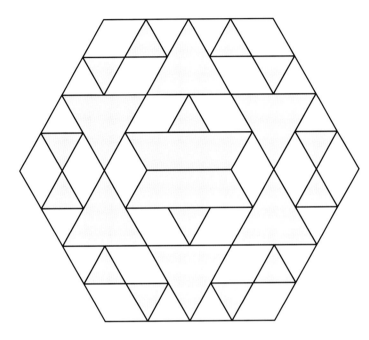

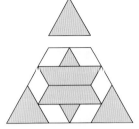

1. Make 1; join.

2. Make 6.

3. Join; make 3.

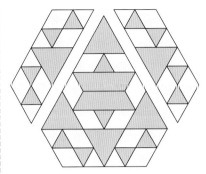

4. Join.

Chillies in the Pond

TECHNIQUES

Hand piecing, page 10

Adding borders, page 15

1. Make 3.

2. Make 3.

3. Join; make 2.

4. Make 1.

5. Join

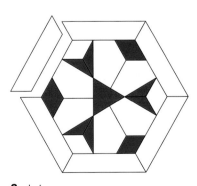

6. Join.

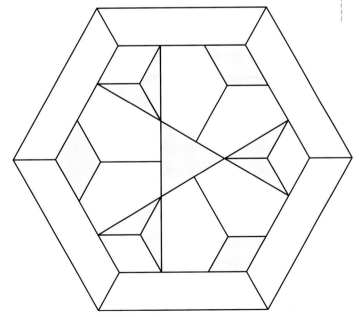

Be My Valentine

TECHNIQUES

Foundation piecing, page 11

Adding borders, page 15

1. Make 1 of each.

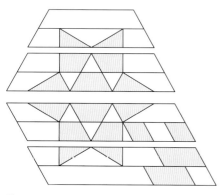

2. Join.

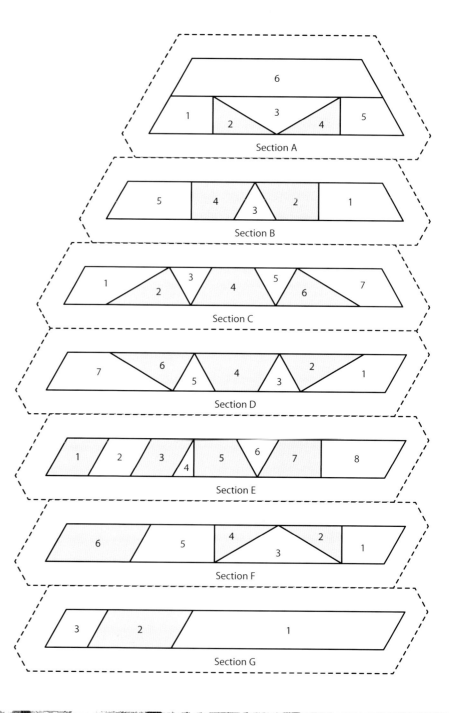

Section A

Section B

Section C

Section D

Section E

Section F

Section G

Hidden Love

TECHNIQUES

Foundation piecing, page 11

Adding borders, page 15

1. Make 1 of each.

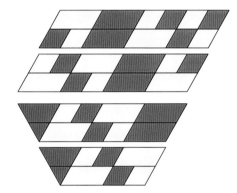

2. Join.

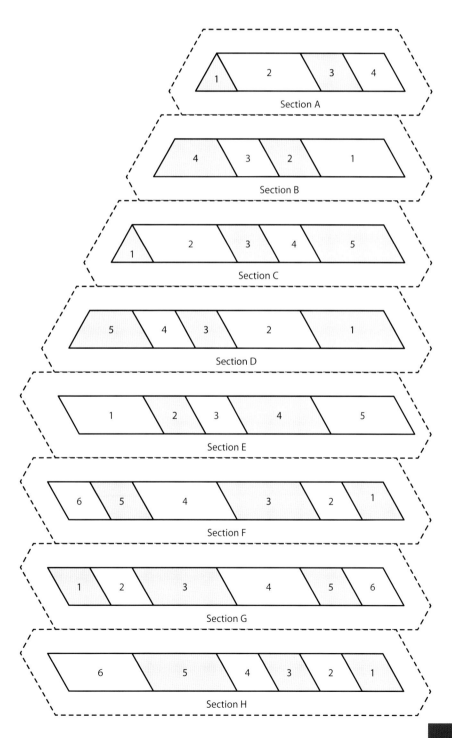

Independence

TECHNIQUES

Hand piecing, page 10

Center stars, page 14

Adding borders, page 15

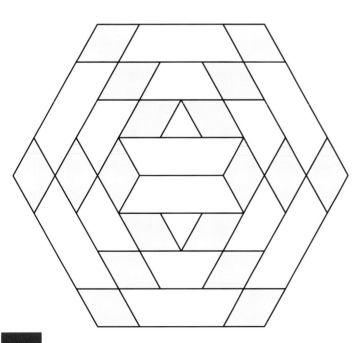

1. Make 3.

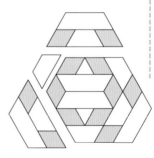

2. Make 1; join.

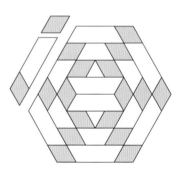

3. Join.

The Vultures Circle

TECHNIQUES

Hand piecing, page 10

Adding borders, page 15

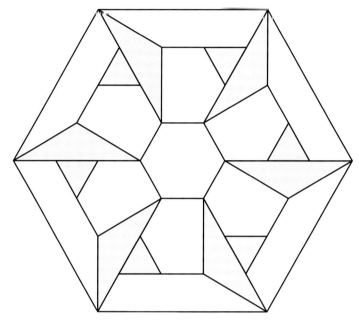

1. Make 6.

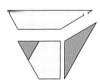

2. Join; make 6.

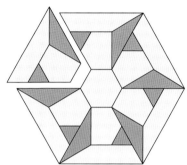

3. Join.

Lightning Ridge

TECHNIQUES

Hand piecing, page 10

Adding borders, page 15

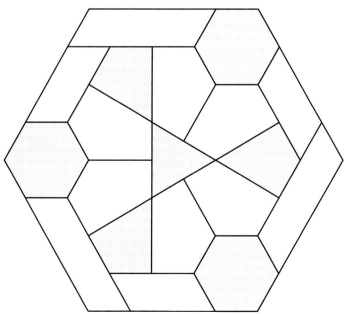

1. Make 3.

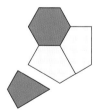

2. Make 2.

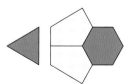

3. Make 1.

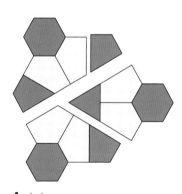

4. Join.

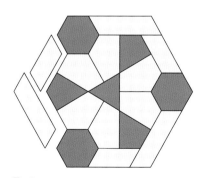

5. Join.

Stars in the Jungle

TECHNIQUES

Hand piecing, page 10

Adding borders, page 15

1. Make 6.

2. Make 2.

6. Join; make 2.

3. Make 1.

4. Make 2.

5. Make 2.

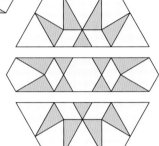

7. Join.

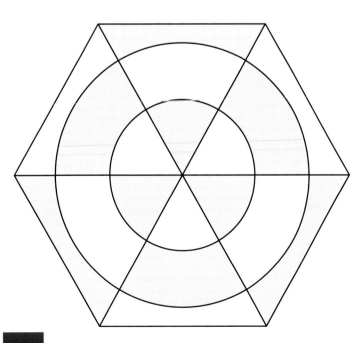

Whirlpool

TECHNIQUES

Hand piecing, page 10

Adding borders, page 15

1. Make 3.

2. Make 3.

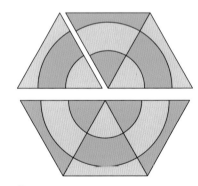

3. Join.

Buttercups

TECHNIQUES

Hand piecing, page 10

Adding borders, page 15

1. Make 6.

2. Join; make 1.

3. Make 2.

4. Make 2.

5. Join; make 2.

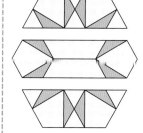

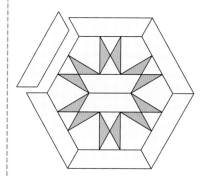

6. Join.

7. Join.

Team Lindsay

TECHNIQUES

Hand piecing, page 10

Partial seams, page 13

Adding borders, page 15

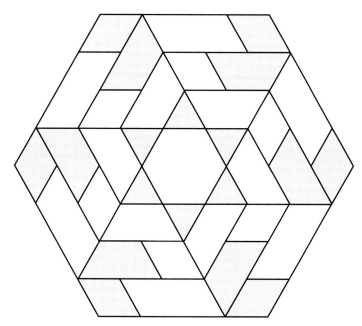

1. Make 6.

2. Make 4.

3. Join; make 2.

4. Make 1 with partial seams.

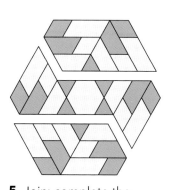

5. Join; complete the partial seams.

Incredible Lives

TECHNIQUES

Hand piecing, page 10

Center stars, page 14

Adding borders, page 15

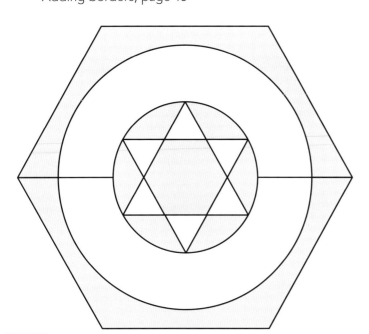

1. Make 1.

2. Join.

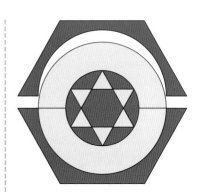

3. Join.

Antipodean

TECHNIQUES

Hand piecing, page 10

Partial seams, page 13

Adding borders, page 15

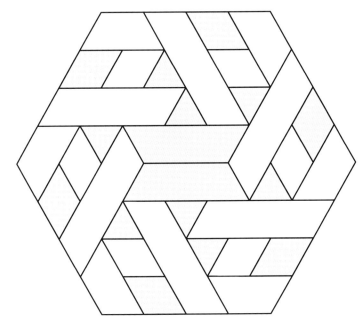

1. Make 6.

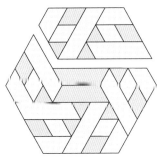

4. Join; complete the partial seam.

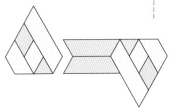

2. Join; make 2.

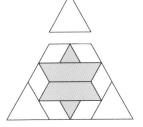

3. Join; make 1 with partial seams.

Lily Pond

TECHNIQUES

Hand piecing, page 10

Center stars, page 14

Adding borders, page 15

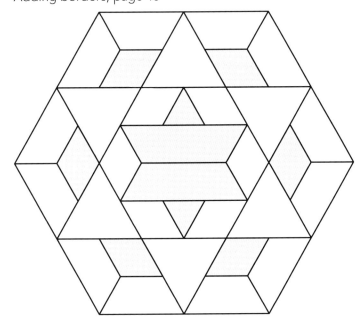

1. Make 1; join.

2. Make 6.

3. Make 3.

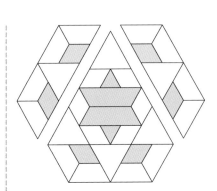

4. Join.

Cherry Pie

TECHNIQUES

Hand piecing, page 10

Adding borders, page 15

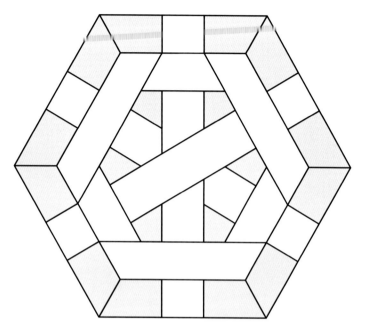

1. Make 2,

2. Make 2.

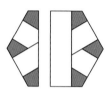

3. Join.

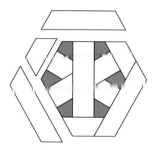

4. Join.

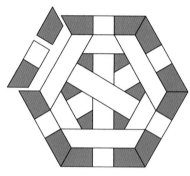

5. Join.

David

TECHNIQUES

Hand piecing, page 10

Adding borders, page 15

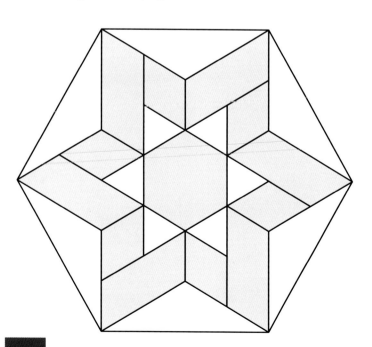

1. Make 6.

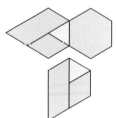

2. Join.

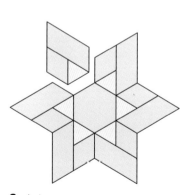

3. Join.

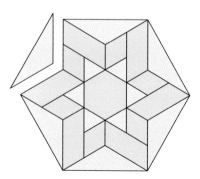

4. Join.

Change

TECHNIQUES

Hand piecing, page 10

Adding borders, page 15

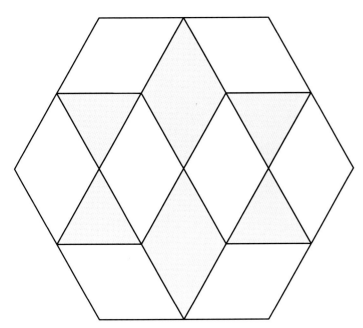

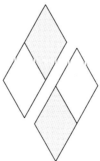

1. Make 1.

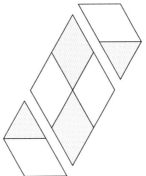

2. Join; make 1.

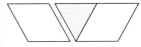

3. Make 2.

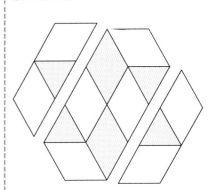

4. Join.

Pacman's Revenge

TECHNIQUES

Hand piecing, page 10

Adding borders, page 15

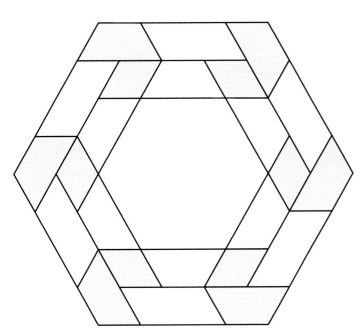

1. Make 3.

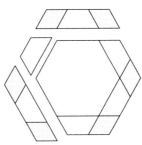

2. Join.

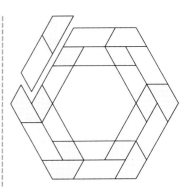

3. Join.

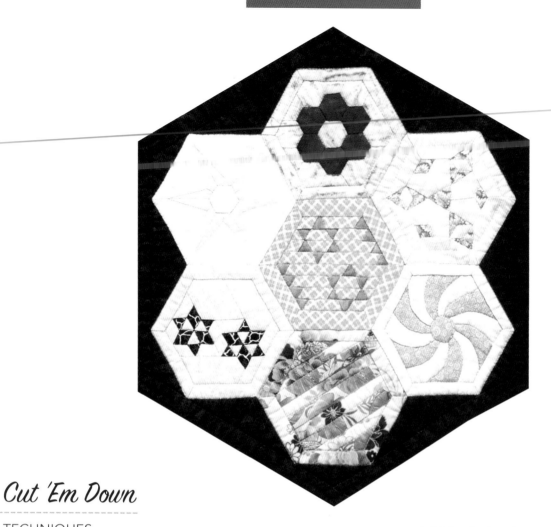

Cut 'Em Down

TECHNIQUES

Foundation piecing, page 11

Adding borders, page 15

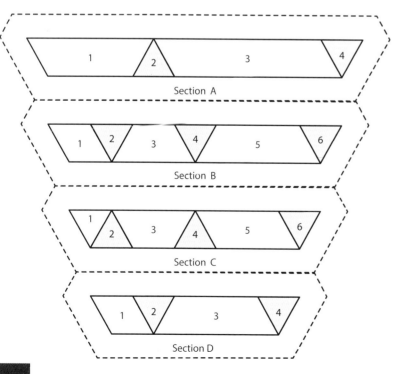

1. Make 2 of each.

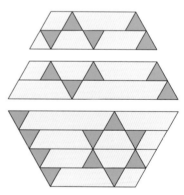

Section A

Section B

Section C

Section D

2. Join.

Grandma's Garden

TECHNIQUES

Hand piecing, page 10

Adding borders, page 15

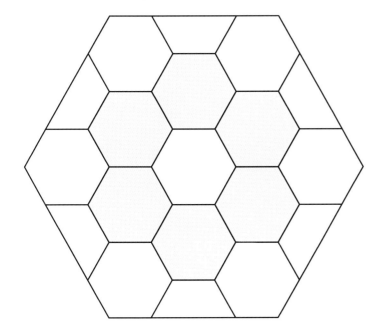

1. Make 1.

2. Make 2.

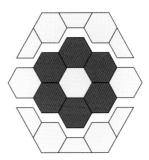

3. Join.

Looking for Isobel

TECHNIQUES

Hand piecing, page 10

Adding borders, page 15

1. Make 3.

2. Make 3.

3. Join; make 2.

4. Make 1.

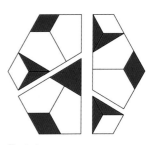

5. Join.

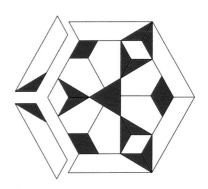

6. Join.

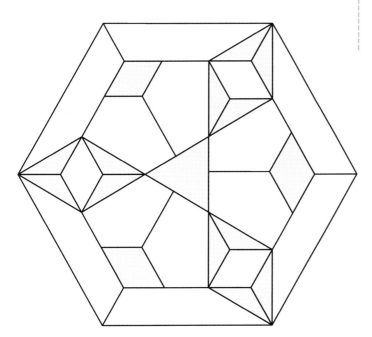

Too Hot

TECHNIQUES

Hand piecing, page 10

Appliqué, page 12

Adding borders, page 15

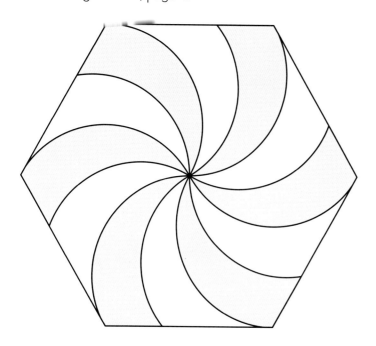

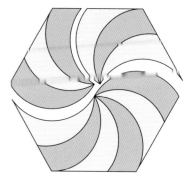

1. Make 2.

2. Make 2.

3. Join.

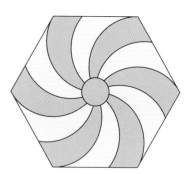

4. Appliqué the circle.

The Theft

TECHNIQUES

Foundation piecing, page 11

Adding borders, page 15

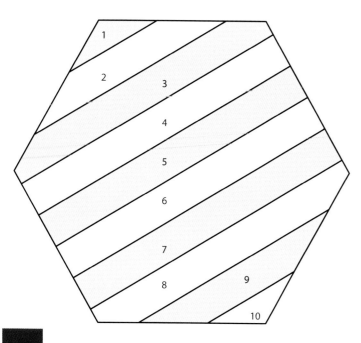

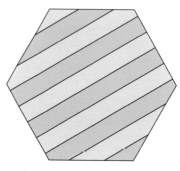

Make 1.

Just the Two of Us

TECHNIQUES

Hand piecing, page 10

Adding borders, page 15

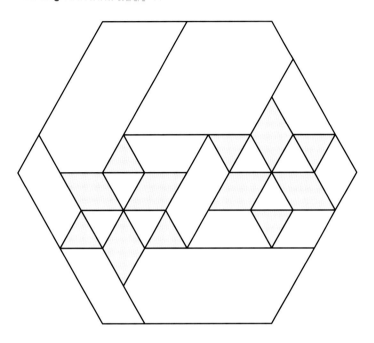

1. Make 2.

2. Join.

3. Join.

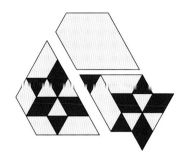

4. Join.

5. Join.

Kendall

TECHNIQUES

Hand piecing, page 10

Adding borders, page 15

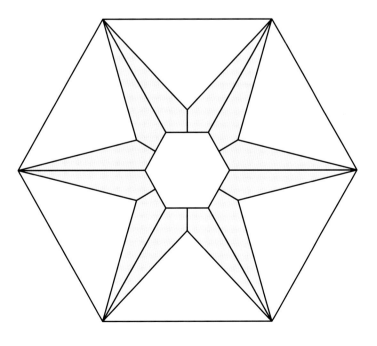

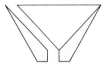

1. Make 6.

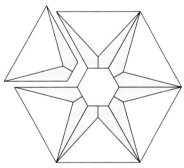

2. Join.

Sunday Brunch

TECHNIQUES

Hand piecing, page 10

Adding borders, page 15

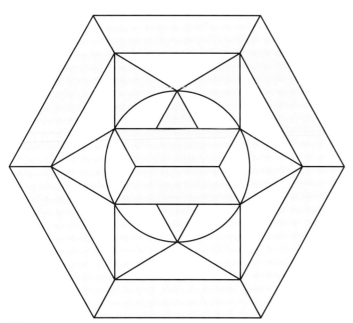

1. Join; make 1.

2. Join; make 2.

3. Join; make 2.

4. Join; make 2.

5. Join.

Morning Dip

TECHNIQUES

Hand piecing, page 10

Adding borders, page 15

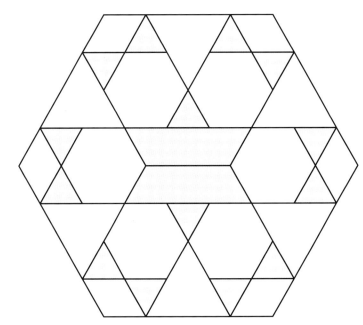

1. Make 6.

2. Join; make 1.

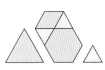

3. Make 2.

4. Make 2.

5. Join; make 2.

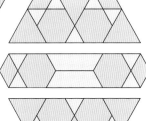

6. Join.

Hold Me Tight

TECHNIQUES

Hand piecing, page 10

Center stars, page 14

Adding borders, page 15

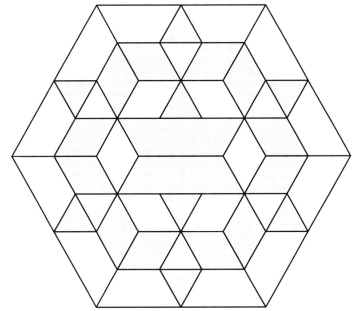

1. Make 1.

2. Make 6.

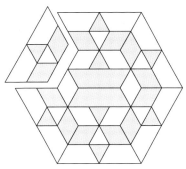

3. Join.

Moving Walls

TECHNIQUES

Foundation piecing, page 11

Adding borders, page 15

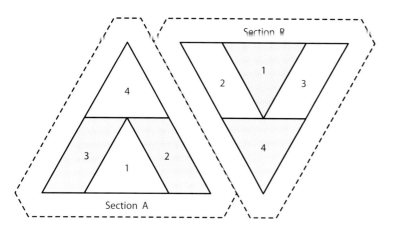

1. Make 3 of each.

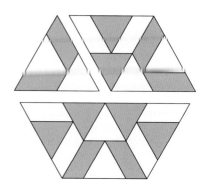

2. Join.

Hotel Taoyuan

TECHNIQUES

Hand piecing, page 10

Adding borders, page 15

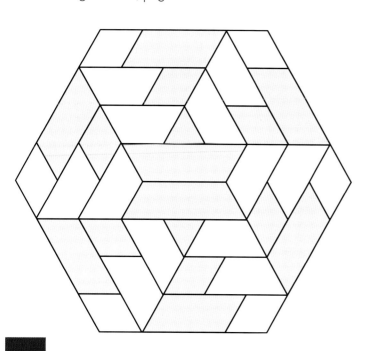

1. Make 6.

2. Join; make 2.

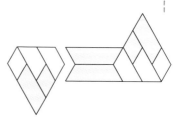

3. Join; make 1.

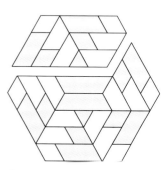

4. Join.

Twisting

TECHNIQUES

Hand piecing, page 10

Adding borders, page 15

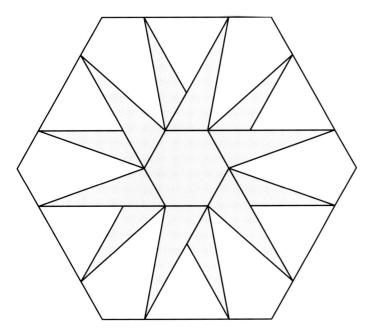

1. Make 6.

2. Make 5.

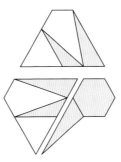

3. Join.

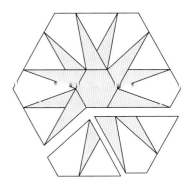

4. Join.

Talking Heads

TECHNIQUES

Hand piecing, page 10

Center stars, page 14

Adding borders, page 15

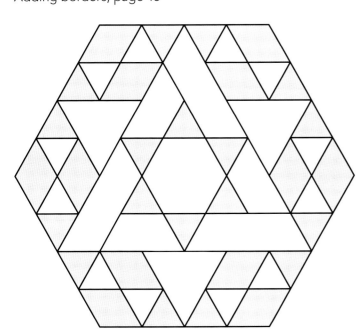

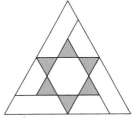

1. Make 1.

2. Make 6.

3. Join; make 3.

4. Join.

Amethyst

TECHNIQUES

Hand piecing, page 10

Adding borders, page 15

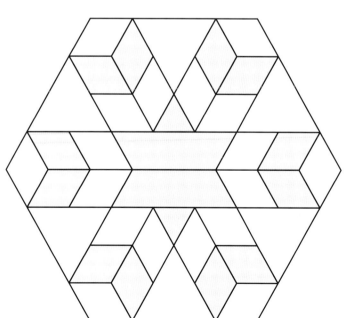

1. Make 1.

2. Make 4.

3. Make 2.

4. Make 2.

5. Join; make 2.

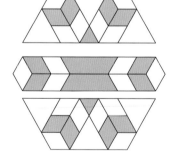

6. Join.

Star Within

TECHNIQUES

Hand piecing, page 10

Center stars, page 11

Adding borders, page 15

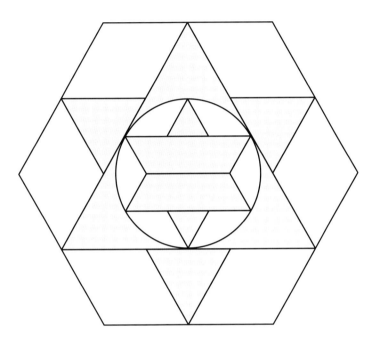

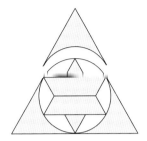

1. Make 1; join.

2. Make 3.

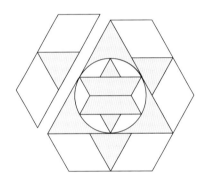

3. Join.

Snow Between the Lakes

TECHNIQUES

Hand piecing, page 10

Adding borders, page 15

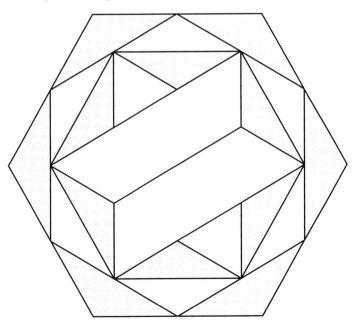

1. Make 2.

2. Join; make 1.

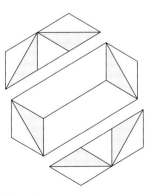

3. Join.

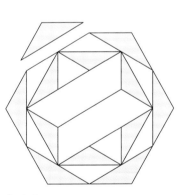

4. Join.

When I Am King

TECHNIQUES

Foundation piecing, page 11

Adding borders, page 15

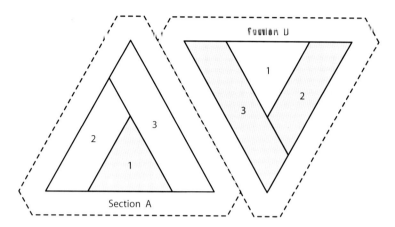

1. Make 3 of each.

2. Join.

Colors of Age

TECHNIQUES

Hand piecing, page 10

Adding borders, page 15

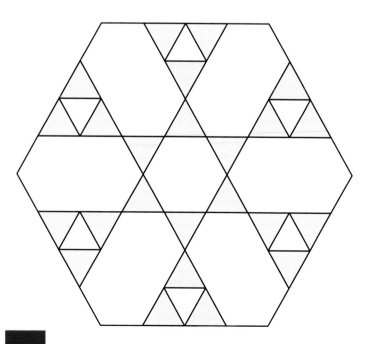

1. Make 6.

2. Make 2.

3. Make 2.

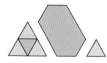

4. Join; make 2.

5. Join; make 1.

6. Join.

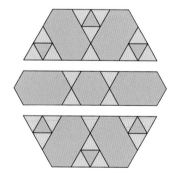

Tail Spin

TECHNIQUES

Hand piecing, page 10

Adding borders, page 15

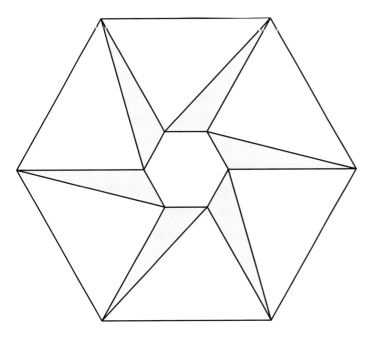

1. Make 6.

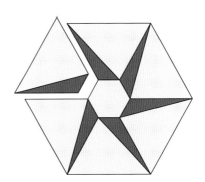

2. Join.

Pretty Maid

TECHNIQUES

Hand piecing, page 10

Adding borders, page 15

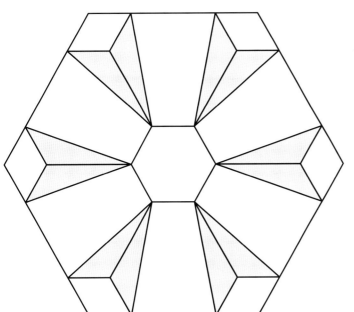

1. Make 6.

2. Make 2.

3. Make 2.

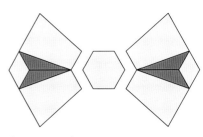

4. Join; make 1.

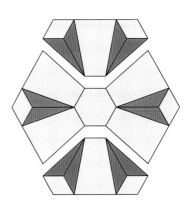

5. Join.

Erica's Bouquet

TECHNIQUES

Hand piecing, page 10

Appliqué, page 12

Adding borders, page 15

Note: The flower spray was fussy cut.

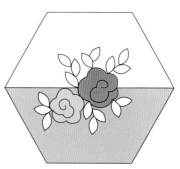

Add appliqué, using your preferred method.

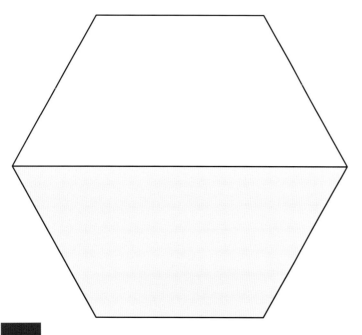

Flight of the Fireflies

TECHNIQUES

Hand piecing, page 10

Partial seams, page 13

Adding borders, page 15

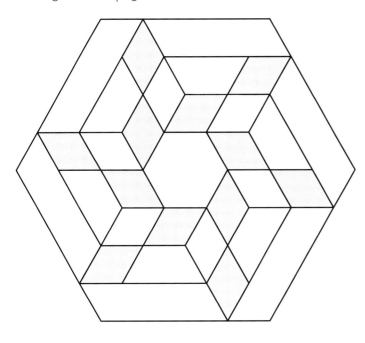

1. Join with partial seams.

2. Make 6.

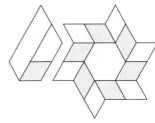

3. Join.

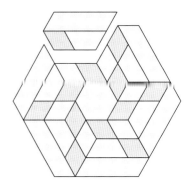

4. Join.

100 Points

TECHNIQUES

Embroidery, page 12

Adding borders, page 15

Satin stitch only the star, using a single strand of Presencia Finca 3670 (teal).

Lifesaver

TECHNIQUES

Hand piecing, page 10

Adding borders, page 15

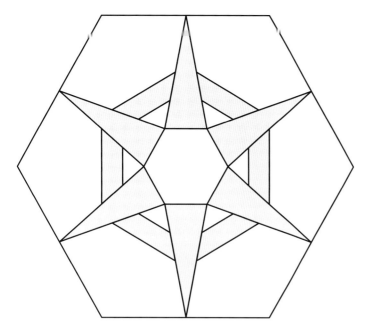

1. Make 6.

2. Make 2.

3. Make 2.

4. Join: make 1

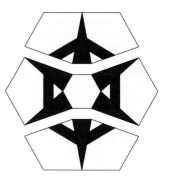

5. Join.

Semaphore Flags

TECHNIQUES

Foundation piecing, page 11

Adding borders, page 15

1. Make 6.

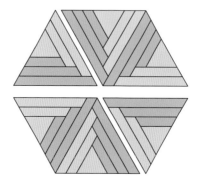

2. Join.

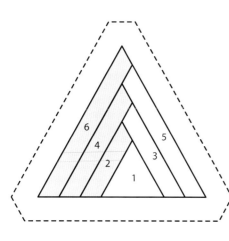

Steeples Abound

TECHNIQUES

Hand piecing, page 10

Adding borders, page 15

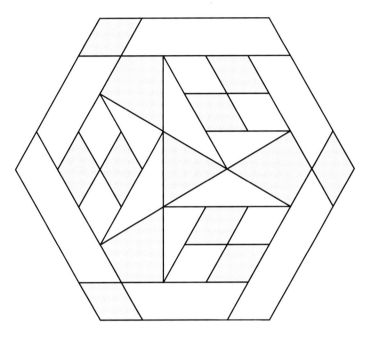

1. Make 3.

2. Make 2.

3. Make 1.

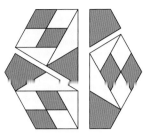

4. Join.

5. Join.

Michelin Babies

TECHNIQUES

Hand piecing, page 10

Appliqué, page 12

Adding borders, page 15

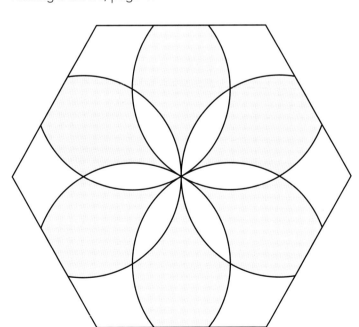

1. Make 3.

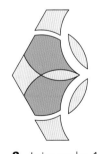

2. Join; make 1.

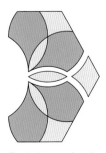

3. Join; make 1.

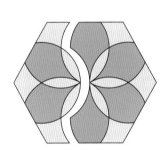

4. Join.

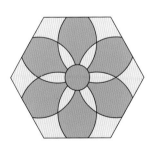

5. Appliqué the circle.

The Jester's Cloak

TECHNIQUES

Foundation piecing, page 11

Adding borders, page 15

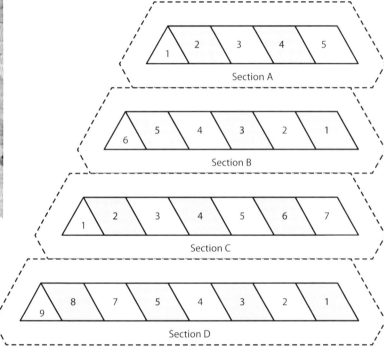

1. Make 1 of each.

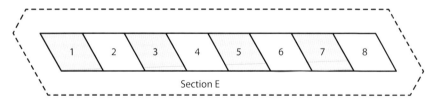

2. Make 4.

3. Join.

Blood from the Dust

TECHNIQUES

Hand piecing, page 10

Center stars, page 14

Adding borders, page 15

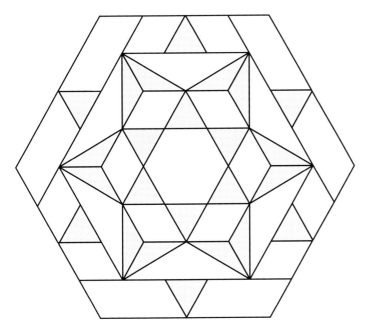

1. Make 6.

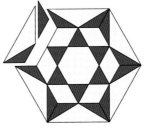

2. Make 1; join.

3. Make 3.

4. Make 3.

5. Join.

Beside the Fountain

TECHNIQUES

Hand piecing, page 10

Adding borders, page 15

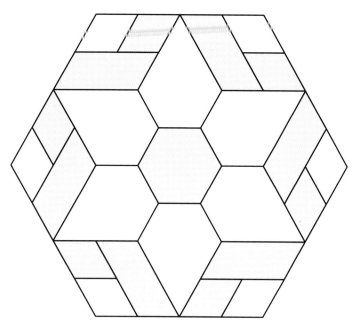

1. Make 6.

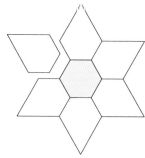

2. Make 1.

3. Join.

Fractured Felines

TECHNIQUES

Hand piecing, page 10

Adding borders, page 15

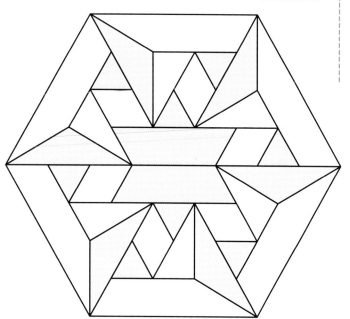

1. Make 2.

2. Join; make 2.

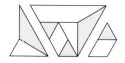

3. Join; make 2.

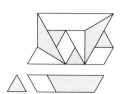

4. Join; make 2.

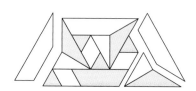

5. Join; make 2.

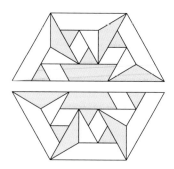

6. Join.

Bygone Days

TECHNIQUES

Hand piecing, page 10

Adding borders, page 15

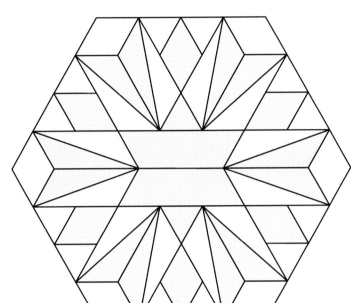

1. Make 6.

5. Join; make 2.

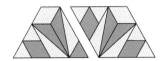

2. Join; make 1.

6. Join; make 2.

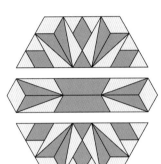

3. Make 6.

4. Join; make 2.

7. Join.

Stars upon the Snow

TECHNIQUES

Hand piecing, page 10

Center stars, page 14

Adding borders, page 15

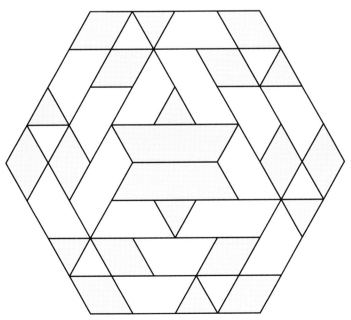

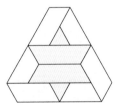

1. Make 1.

2. Make 3.

4. Join.

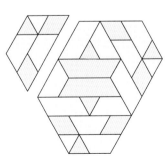

3. Join.

Fred and Ginger

TECHNIQUES

Hand piecing, page 10

Adding borders, page 15

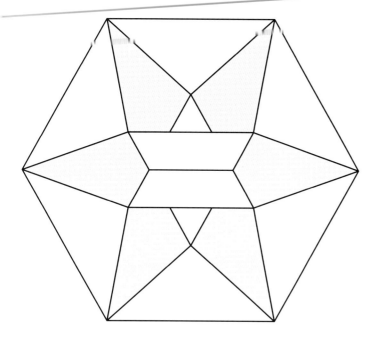

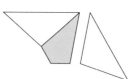

1. Make 2.

2. Make 2.

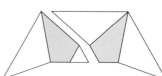

3. Join; make 2.

4. Make 1.

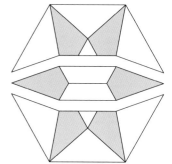

5. Join.

Jellyfish Swirl

TECHNIQUES

Hand piecing, page 10

Adding borders, page 15

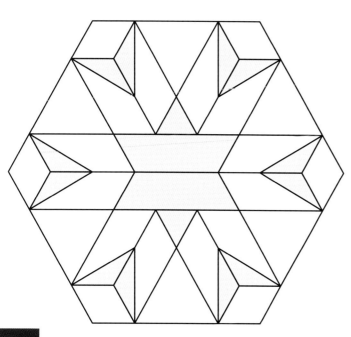

1. Make 1.

2. Make 4.

3. Make 2.

4. Make 2.

5. Join; make 2.

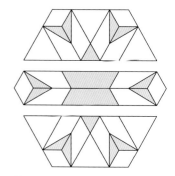

6. Join.

Friday Night Flowers

TECHNIQUES

Hand piecing, page 10

Adding borders, page 15

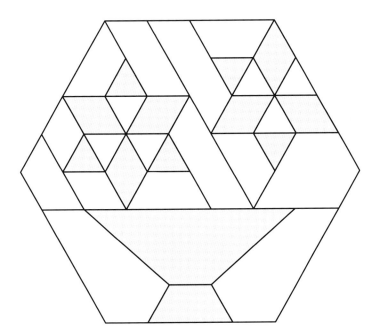

1. Make 2.

2. Join; make 2.

3. Join; make 1.

4. Join; make 1.

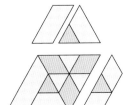

5. Join.

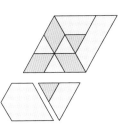

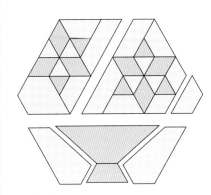

50 and Loving It!

TECHNIQUES

Hand piecing, page 10

Adding borders, page 15

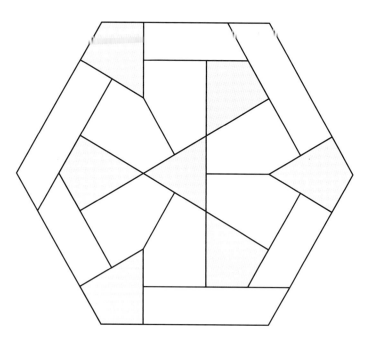

1. Make 3.

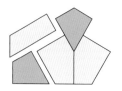

2. Make 2.

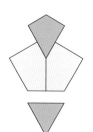

3. Make 1.

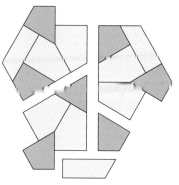

4. Join.

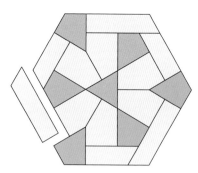

5. Join.

Inspirations

TECHNIQUES

Hand piecing, page 10

Center stars, page 14

Adding borders, page 15

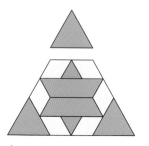

1. Make 1; join.

2. Make 3.

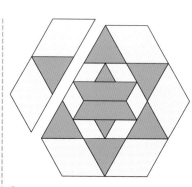

3. Join.

Fields Lay Fallow

TECHNIQUES

Hand piecing, page 10

Adding borders, page 15

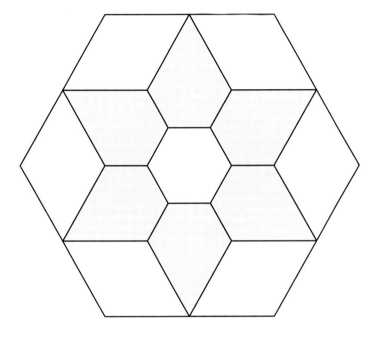

1. Make 3.

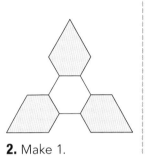

2. Make 1.

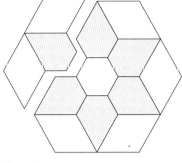

3. Join.

Peacock Pride

TECHNIQUES

Hand piecing, page 10

Adding borders, page 15

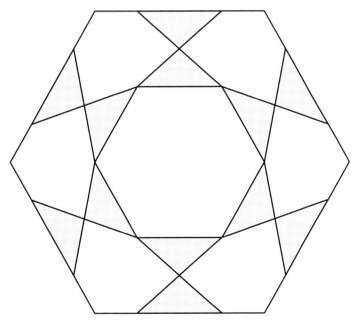

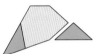

1. Make 2.

2. Make 2.

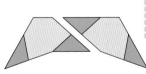

3. Join; make 2.

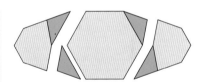

4. Join; make 1.

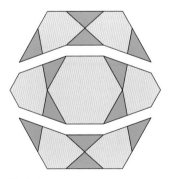

5. Join.

Over the Headland

TECHNIQUES

Hand piecing, page 10

Adding borders, page 15

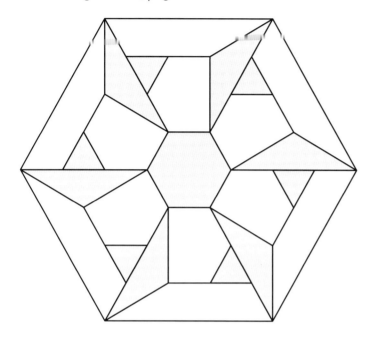

1. Make 6.

2. Join; make 6.

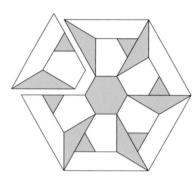

3. Join.

Sneezing

TECHNIQUES

Hand piecing, page 10

Center stars, page 14

Adding borders, page 15

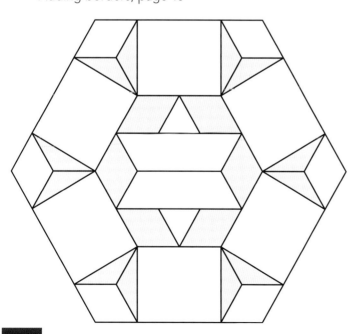

1. Make 1.

2. Make 6.

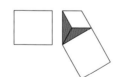

3. Make 2.

4. Make 2.

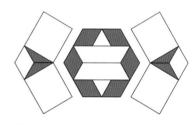

5. Join; make 1.

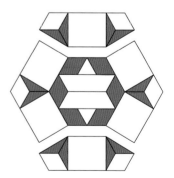

6. Join.

Star Jump

TECHNIQUES

Hand piecing, page 10

Adding borders, page 15

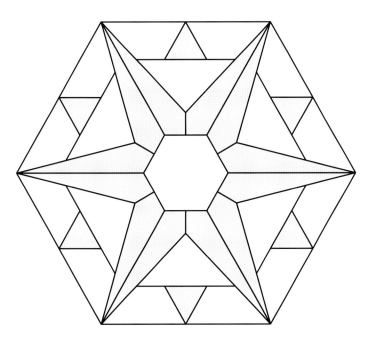

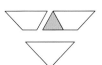

1. Make 6.

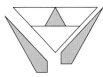

2. Join; make 6.

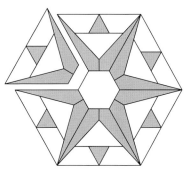

3. Join.

Child's Bouquet

TECHNIQUES

Hand piecing, page 10

Adding borders, page 15

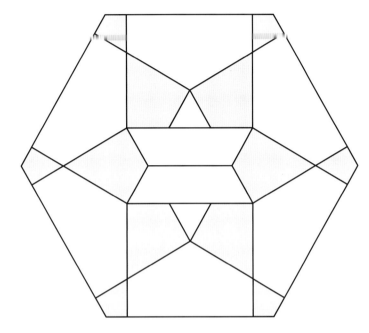

1. Make 4.

2. Make 2.

3. Make 2.

4. Join; make 2.

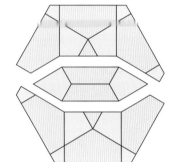

5. Make 1.

6. Join.

Celtic Gem

TECHNIQUES

Hand piecing, page 10

Adding borders, page 15

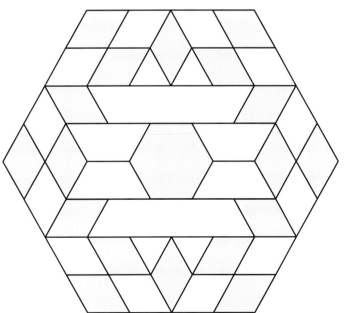

1. Make 6.

2. Make 2.

3. Join; make 2.

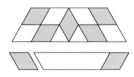

4. Join, make 2.

5. Make 1.

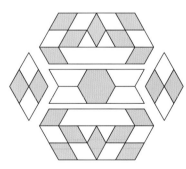

6. Join.

Country Sampler

TECHNIQUES

Hand piecing, page 10

Center stars, page 14

Adding borders, page 15

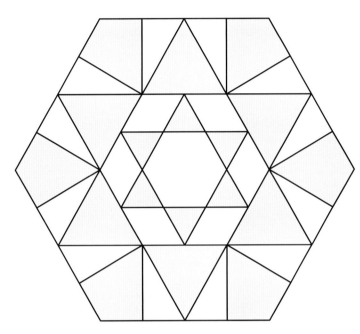

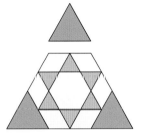

1. Make 1; join.

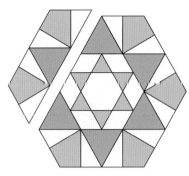

4. Join.

2. Make 3.

3. Join, make 3.

Spring in Blossom

TECHNIQUES

Hand piecing, page 10

Center stars, page 14

Adding borders, page 15

1. Make 1.

2. Make 6.

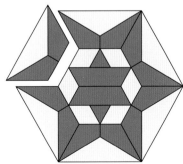

3. Join.

Chilled Gazpachos

TECHNIQUES

Hand piecing, page 10

Center stars, page 14

Adding borders, page 15

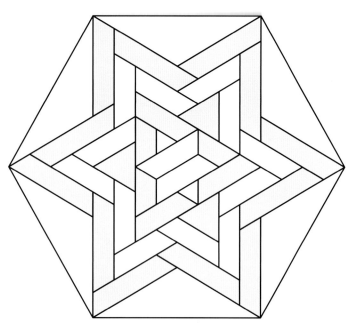

1. Make 3.

2. Make 1; join.

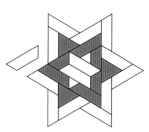

3. Join.

4. Join.

5. Join.

Facing the Sun

TECHNIQUES

Hand piecing, page 10

Center stars, page 14

Adding borders, page 15

1. Make 1; join.

2. Make 3.

3. Make 3.

4. Join; make 3.

5. Join.

Dappled Light

TECHNIQUES

Hand piecing, page 10

Adding borders, page 15

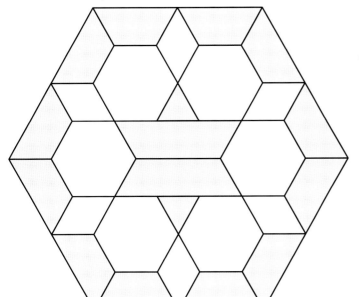

1. Make 6.

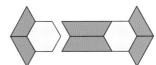

2. Join; make 1.

3. Make 2.

4. Make 2.

5. Join; make 2.

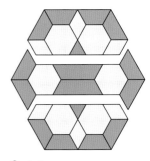

6. Join.

Pink Tutu

TECHNIQUES

Hand piecing, page 10

Center stars, page 14

Adding borders, page 15

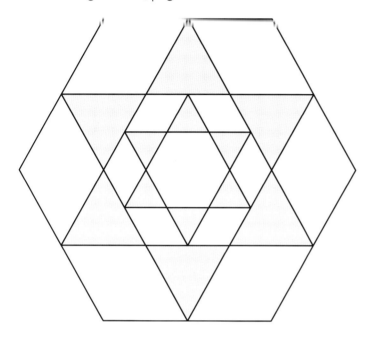

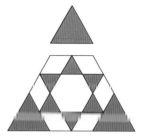

1. Make 1; join.

2. Make 3.

3. Join.

From All Sides

TECHNIQUES

Hand piecing, page 10

Adding borders, page 15

1. Make 6.

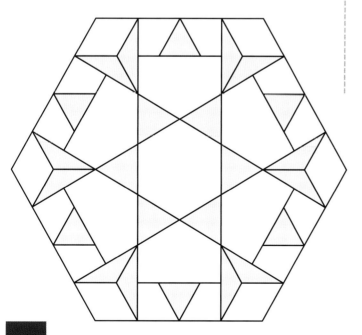

2. Join; make 1.

3. Make 6.

4. Join; make 2.

5. Join; make 2.

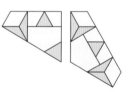

6. Join; make 2.

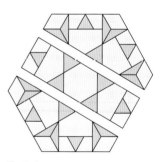

7. Join.

Box Pleats and Windsor Ties

TECHNIQUES

Hand piecing, page 10

Adding borders, page 15

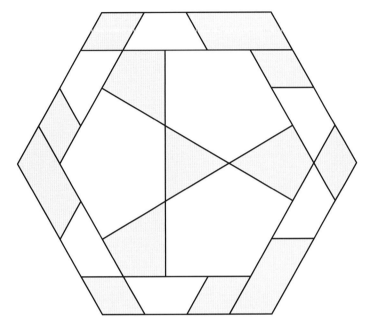

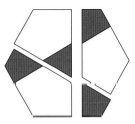

1. Join.

2. Make 3.

3. Join.

Oh Where?

TECHNIQUES

Hand piecing, page 10

Adding borders, page 15

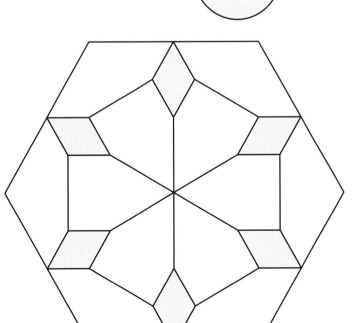

1. Make 6.

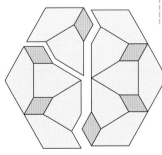

2. Join.

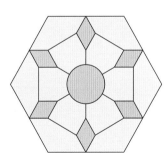

3. Join.

Carefree Bubbles

TECHNIQUES

Hand piecing, page 10

Appliqué, page 12

Adding borders, page 15

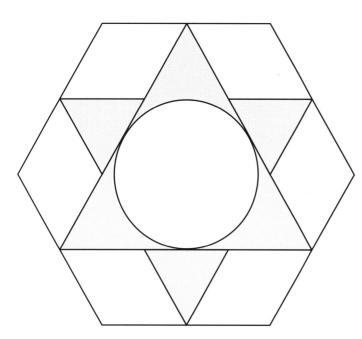

1. Make 3.

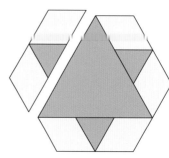

2. Join.

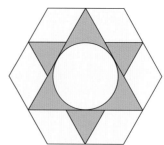

3. Appliqué the circle.

Quiet Reflections

TECHNIQUES

Hand piecing, page 10

Adding borders, page 15

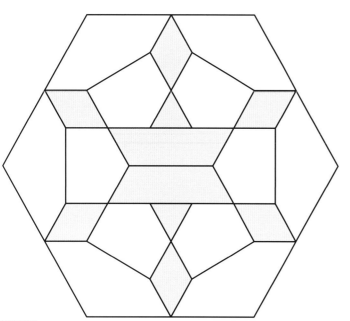

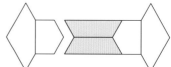

1. Make 1.

2. Make 2.

3. Make 2.

4. Join; make 2.

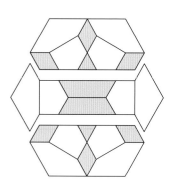

5. Join.

Smiling in Red

TECHNIQUES

Hand piecing, page 10

Adding borders, page 15

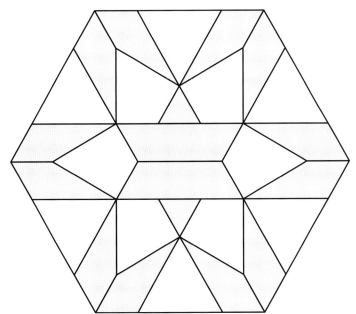

1. Make 6.

2. Join; make 1.

3. Make 2.

4. Make 2.

5. Join; make 2.

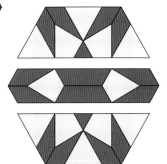

6. Join.

Python Feast

TECHNIQUES

Hand piecing, page 10

Adding borders, page 15

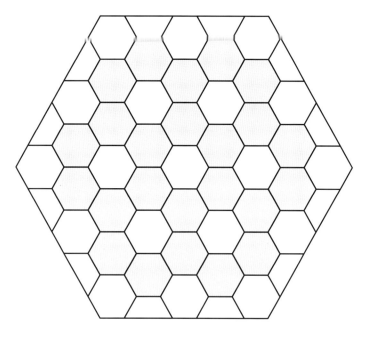

1. Make 1.

2. Make 4.

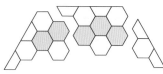

3. Join; make 2.

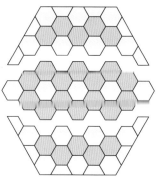

4. Join.

Put 'Em Up

TECHNIQUES

Hand piecing, page 10

Center stars, page 14

Adding borders, page 15

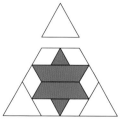

1. Make 1; join.

2. Make 6.

3. Make 3.

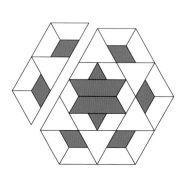

4. Join.

Blueberry Pie

TECHNIQUES

Hand piecing, page 10

Adding borders, page 15

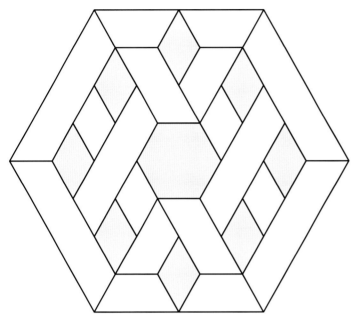

1. Make 2.

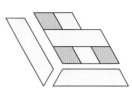

2. Join; make 2.

4. Make 2.

5. Join; make 2.

3. Join; make 1.

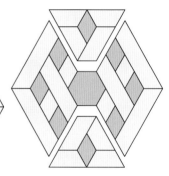

6. Join.

Coming and Going

TECHNIQUES

Hand piecing, page 10

Adding borders, page 15

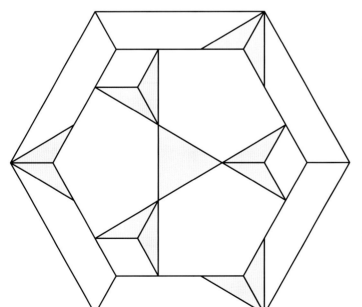

1. Make 3.

2. Make 2.

3. Join; make 2.

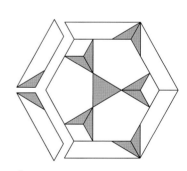

4. Join.

Garden Party

TECHNIQUES

Machine piecing

Trimming oversize blocks, page 13

Adding borders, page 15

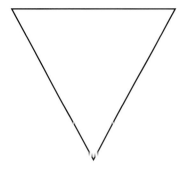

Cut 9 strips ¾″ × 10″.

Seams are a stitch larger than ¼″; the finished width of the joined strips is 2⅜″.

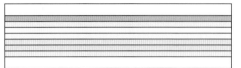

1. Join the strips along the long sides, and press seams in one direction.

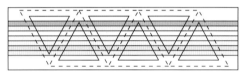

2. Cut 6 sections.

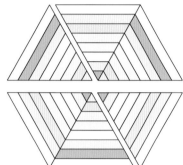

3. Join.

A New Kingdom

TECHNIQUES

Foundation piecing, page 11

Adding borders, page 15

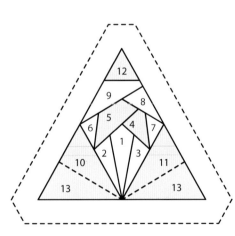

1. Make 6, sewing up to Fabric 12 *only*.

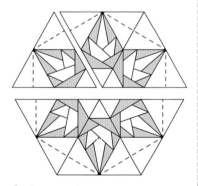

2. Join, and press.

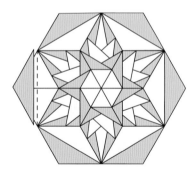

3. Sew Fabric 13 into place.

Tim Tam Evidence

TECHNIQUES

Foundation piecing, page 11

Adding borders, page 15

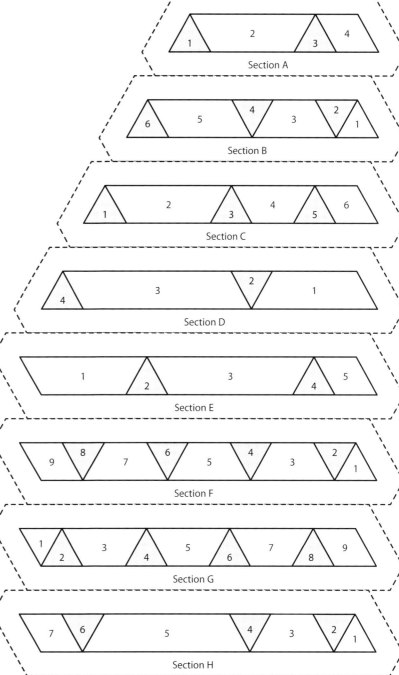

Section A

Section B

Section C

Section D

Section E

Section F

Section G

Section H

1. Make 1 of each.

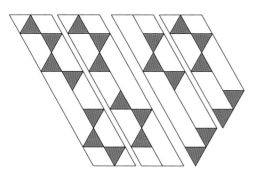

2. Join.

Completing the Quilt

LAYOUT

1. On a design wall or floor, lay out all the collections to obtain a pleasing arrangement. Take care that the collections are oriented correctly, with every long frame lying against a short frame. Ensure that the following have extension frames (see Completing a Full Collection with Extension, page 16):

- Collections 8, 21, 34, and 47 have an extension frame on the left-hand edge.
- Collections 13, 26, 39, and 52 have an extension frame on the right-hand edge.

2. Mark the top of each collection with a numbered tag and safety pin.

3. Photograph your layout for future reference.

Quilt layout

QUILTING

Quilting the Collections

MATERIALS

To quilt 1 collection:

- 1 completed collection

- Batting: 16″ × 16″ square
  (8″ × 16″ for side and corner collections)

- Backing: 16″ × 16″ square
  (8″ × 16″ for side and corner collections)

CONSTRUCTION

Raconteur is completed using the quilt-as-you-go technique. You will complete each collection before joining it to the other collections.

1. Press the backing fabric. Place it right side down on a flat surface, and tape firmly.

2. Smooth out the batting over the backing. Place the pieced collection on top, right side up.

3. Baste securely with safety pins placed 3″ apart.

4. Stitch-in-the-ditch each featured fabric piece and the borders, but be sure *not* to quilt in the outer frame area.

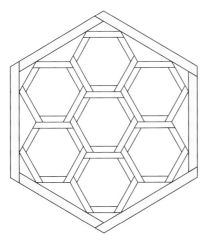

Be sure *not* to quilt in outer frame area.

Joining the Collections

1. Press the quilted collection. The collection top is the *finished size with a ¼″ seam allowance*.

2. Pin the backing completely out of the way, making sure *not* to trim it. Place the quilted collection on a cutting mat, and trim the batting *only*, making it even with the collection top.

3. Unpin the backing. Lay the quilted collection face up on the cutting mat to trim the backing. Trim the *backing fabric ¾″* larger than the collection top on all sides.

4. Mark the joining sides of 2 neighboring collections with a pin.

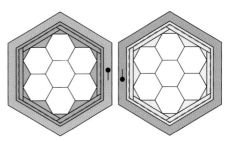

Mark with pins.

5. Place the 2 collections together, right sides together. Pin the batting and backing of the top collection out of the way of the seam about to be sewn.

6. Stitch together on the marked line. In the seam, there should be 1 backing, 1 batting, and 2 collection tops.

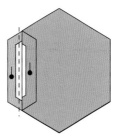

Stitch.

7. Trim even with the collection edge and press the seam allowance outward.

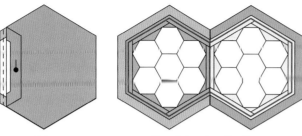

Trim.   Two joined collections

8. Pin the backing back and trim any *overlapping batting* even with the neighboring edge.

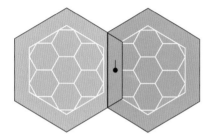

Trim overlapping batting.

9. Select a collection that neighbors the 2 joined collections.

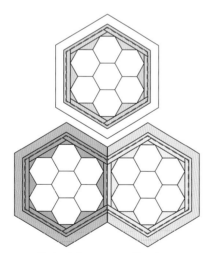

Select the next collection.

10. From the joined collections, trim the excess *backing* even with the top *only* on the sides to be joined next.

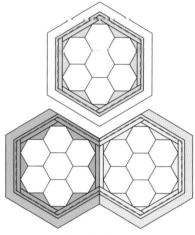

Trim backing.

11. Mark the seam allowance ¼˝ from both ends.

12. Stitch on the marked line between the ¼˝ points.

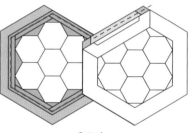

Stitch.

13. Open the collections and press the seam allowance to one side.

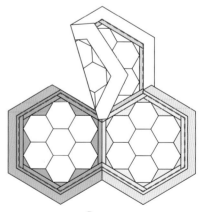

Press.

14. Trim any *overlapping batting* level with the neighboring edge.

15. With right sides of the collections together, the raw edges matching, and the excess batting and backing pinned out of the way, stitch from the edge of the collection to the ¼˝ point and backstitch. Press.

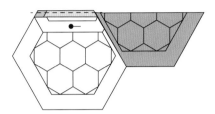

Stitch together.

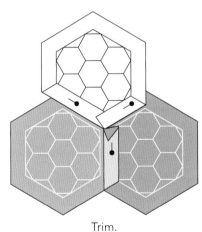

Three joined collections

16. Trim the excess fabric at the intersection.

Trim.

17. Turn a ¼˝ hem on the excess backing fabric, and slipstitch in place, covering the previous seamline.

18. On the back, check to see if the 3 seams meet. If they do not, you may choose to appliqué a circle over the corner to hide this.

Slipstitch backing.

19. Turning to the top of the quilt, stitch in the previous seamline, using matching thread.

Quilting the Borders

The inner borders are added to the joined quilt top and quilted through the batting at the same time as being sewn to the quilt top.

The middle and outer borders are quilted separately before being joined to the quilt. These borders are cut 2˝–6˝ longer than the finished size to allow for shrinkage while quilting. The more quilting, the greater the shrinkage.

MATERIALS

• First border: ⅓ yard

• Middle border: 1¼ yards

• Outer border: 2¾ yards

• Border backing: 4½ yards

• Batting: 1½ yards

CUTTING

WOF = width of fabric

First border

- Cut 6 strips 1¼″ × WOF. From 1 strip, subcut 2 strips 1¼″ × 18″. Join the remaining 5 strips end to end; subcut 2 strips 1¼″ × 86″.

Middle border

- Cut 10 strips 3½″ × WOF. Join all 10 strips end to end; subcut 2 strips 3½″ × 90″, 2 strips 3½″ × 56″, and 4 strips 3½″ × 22″.

Outer border

- Cut 5 strips 7½″ × WOF. Join all 5 strips end to end; subcut 2 strips 7½″ × 95″ for side borders.

- Cut 6 strips 5″ × WOF. Join all 6 strips end to end; subcut 2 strips 5″ × 70″ and 4 strips 5″ × 20″ for top, bottom, and angled borders.

- Cut 11 strips 2″ × WOF for binding.

Backing

Backing is cut approximately 1″ larger on all sides than the top fabric.

- Cut 6 strips 3″ × WOF. Join all 6 strips end to end; subcut 2 strips 3″ × 20″ and 2 strips 3″ × 88″ for inner borders.

- Cut 10 strips 5″ × WOF. Join all 10 strips end to end; subcut 2 strips 5″ × 92″, subcut 2 strips 5″ × 58″, and subcut 4 strips 5″ × 24″ for middle borders.

- Cut 5 strips 9½″ × WOF. Join all 5 strips end to end; subcut 2 strips 9½″ × 97″ for side outer borders.

- Cut 6 strips 7″ × WOF. Join all 6 strips end to end; subcut 2 strips 7″ × 72″ and 4 strips 7″ × 22″ for top, bottom, and angled outer borders.

Batting

- Cut 3 strips ¾″ × 100″; subcut 2 strips ¾″ × 88″ and 2 strips ¾″ × 20″ for inner borders.

- Cut 4 strips 4″ × 100″; subcut 2 strips 4″ × 92″, 2 strips 4″ × 58″, and 4 strips 4″ × 24″ for middle borders.

- Cut 2 strips 8″ × 100″; subcut 2 strips 8″ × 95″ for the side outer borders.

- Cut 3 strips 5″ × 100″; subcut 2 strips 5″ × 72″ and 4 strips 5″ × 22″ for the top, bottom, and angled outer borders.

CONSTRUCTION

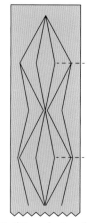

Quilting design for middle borders

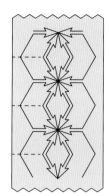

Quilting design for narrow outer borders

Quilting design for wide outer borders

Seam allowances are ¼″.

1. Matching the centers, pin the border fabric to the batting and backing for the middle and outer border fabrics. Make 16 sets.

2. From Quilting Designs (page 243), copy and repeat the quilting design to the required length onto quilting paper using a mechanical pencil.

3. Do the number of repeats given below.

	Angled border	Short borders	Side borders
Middle border	3	11	20
Outer border	5	26	43

4. Matching the centers, securely pin the drawn quilting design to the corresponding fabric. It may be necessary to slightly vary the repeat length of some designs, depending on your quilt size.

5. Using a walking foot and matching thread color, quilt all the border sections. Test a sample before quilting the actual fabric to ensure there is no transfer of pencil lead to the fabric.

Attaching the Borders

Each quilted border, except for the inner border, is added in turn using a method similar to Joining the Collections (page 237). Measure the quilt top; the opposite sides should be the same length. If they differ, find the average of the lengths and make both borders this length.

Inner Border

The first border is added only to the angled and side edges of the quilt.

1. Sew a long basting stitch along the edge of the completed quilt top.

2. Aligning the raw edges and midpoints, place a 1″ × 18″ border strip right side down on the quilt top along the angled edge. Place a 3″ × 20″ backing strip right side up on the underside of the quilt top.

3. Sew together the border, quilt top, and backing layers. Press the border fabric outward. Trim even with the neighboring edges.

4. Pin a ¾″ × 20″ batting strip between the border fabrics. Baste.

5. Aligning the raw edges and midpoints, place a 1¼″ × 90″ border strip right side down on the long sides of the quilt top. Place a 3″ × 92″ backing strip right side up on the underside of the quilt top.

6. Sew together the border, quilt top, and backing layers. Press the border fabric outward.

7. Pin a ¾″ × 92″ batting strip between the border fabrics. Baste.

8. Trim the backing fabric even with the border fabric. Trim the ends even with the neighboring edges.

Optional: The same frame fabric from Collection 7 was used at the top of the inner right-hand side border. If desired, join a 1¼″ × 12″ contrast strip to the top of the inner strip using a 60° seam. Trim the seams, and press toward the dark fabric. Align this with the join and complete as above.

Middle Border

1. *After* quilting, cut the top fabric 3″ wide, centering the design. Pin the backing and batting out of the way as needed.

2. Cut the batting ¼″ less than this measurement on both long sides.

3. Cut the backing 4½″ wide.

4. Complete, following the steps in Joining the Collections (page 237).

5. Attach the top and bottom borders first, then the angled borders, then the side borders.

6. After attaching all the borders, quilt parallel lines ½″ apart in the unquilted areas.

Outer Angled and Top and Bottom Borders

1. *After quilting*, cut the top fabric 3½″ wide, centering the design. Pin the backing and batting out of the way as needed.

2. Cut the batting ¼″ less than this measurement on both long sides.

3. Cut the backing 5″ wide.

4. Complete, following the steps in Joining the Collections (page 237).

5. Attach the top and bottom borders first, then the angled borders.

Outer Side Borders

1. *After quilting*, cut the top fabric 6¾″ wide, centering the design. Pin the backing and batting out of the way as needed.

2. Cut the batting ¼″ less than this measurement on both long sides.

3. Cut the backing 8″ wide.

4. Complete, following the steps in Joining the Collections (page 237).

5. After attaching all the borders to the quilt, echo quilt the outer lines of the design, ½″ apart in the unquilted areas.

Attaching the Binding

1. Join the binding strips with diagonal seams to make one length.

2. Trim the seams to ¼″, and press open.

3. Fold the strip in half, wrong sides together and long edges matching. Press.

4. Leaving a 6″ loose end of binding, with raw edges together and starting partway along one side, stitch the binding to the edge of the quilt with a ¼″ seam.

5. Stop ¼″ from the corner, backstitch, and fold the binding back at a 60° angle.

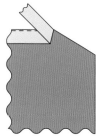

Fold back.

6. With the raw edges together, fold the binding along the next side. Stitch.

Turn corner.

7. Continue to machine stitch the binding around the quilt top, matching the raw edges and mitering the corners as you go.

8. On the last side, stop sewing 16″ from the starting point.

9. Make a 45° fold at the end of the starting strip and press.

10. Lay the folded strip end onto the other end. Mark the fold on the other end.

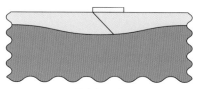

Fold end.

11. Move the binding strips away from the quilt. Match the fold line and the drawn line, and sew them together.

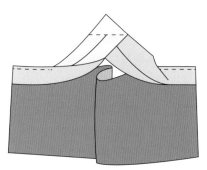

Join binding ends.

12. Trim the seam to ¼″. Press the seam open, and refold the binding.

13. Finish sewing the binding to the quilt top.

14. Trim the batting and backing ¼″ beyond the edge of the quilt top.

15. Fold the binding to the back and slipstitch it neatly in place.

QUILTING DESIGNS

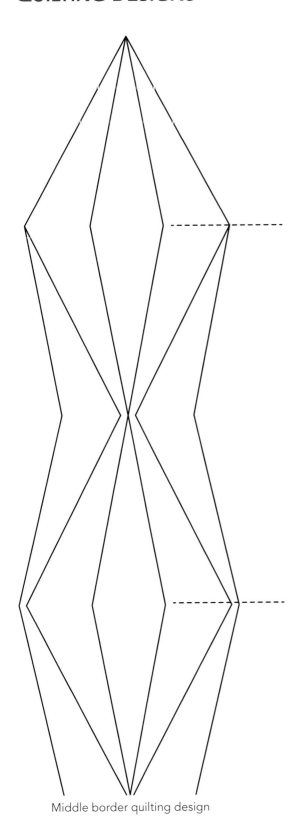

Middle border quilting design

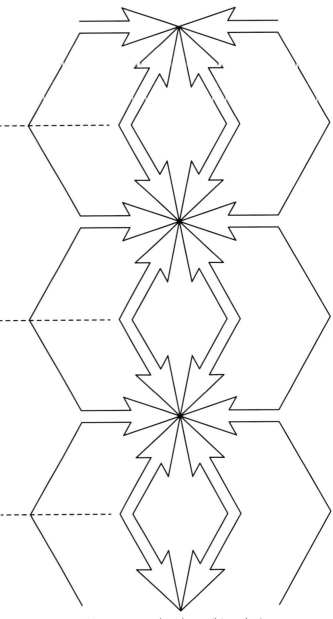

Narrow outer border quilting design

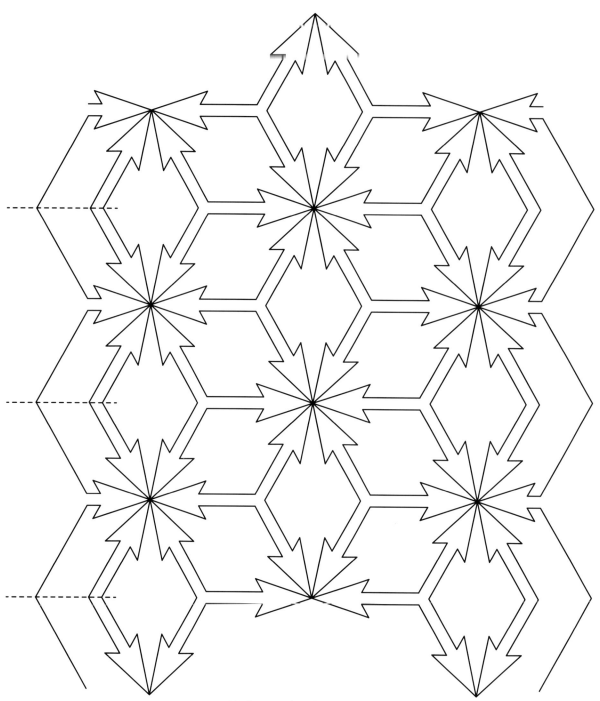

Wide outer border quilting design

Gallery

Beneath the Southern Cross 54″ × 72″, designed by Cinzia White, pieced by Nowra Quilters, quilted by Maxine Sandry of Quilts to the Max, 2017

Blocks are at 100%, 141%, and 250%.

Tall Tales 60″ × 75″, by Cinzia White, 2017

Blocks are at 141%.

Snippets 15¾″ × 13½″, by Cinzia White, 2012

Blocks are at 100%.

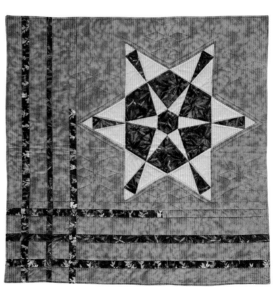

Catch a Falling Star 36″ × 36½″, by Joy L. Cook, 2018

Blocks are at 400%.

Cinzia's Delight   14½″ × 37¼″, by Carol LeMaitre, 2015

Blocks are at 100%.

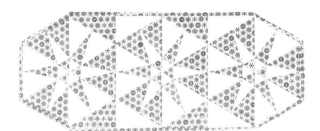

Snow Flakes   38″ × 15¼″, designed by Cinzia White, made by Delma Elliott, 2018

Blocks are at 400%.

Scattered Footpath   13¼″ × 31¾″, by Carol LeMaitre, 2016

Blocks are at 100%.

This Way Please   38″ × 15″, designed by Cinzia White, made by Margaret Di Salvio, 2017

Blocks are at 400%.

Raconteur in Pink, Collection 8   12½″ × 14½″, designed by Cinzia White, made by Margaret McCaughey, 2015

Blocks are at 100%.

Homecoming   40″ × 13½″, designed by Cinzia White, made by Margaret Di Salvio, 2018

Blocks are at 400%.

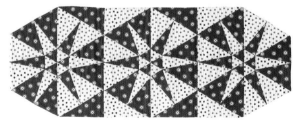

Sew Spotty   37″ × 14¼″, designed by Cinzia White, made by Jannette Jackson, 2018

Blocks are at 400%.

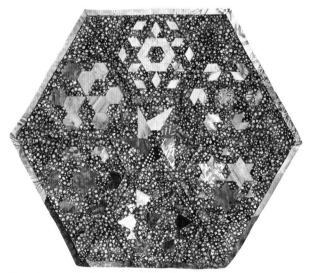

Kaleidoscopic Tales   24″ × 20¾″, designed by Cinzia White, made by Danni Reynolds, 2018

Blocks are at 141%.

About the Author

Cinzia White has been quilting for more than 30 years. She has published numerous patterns in most Australian patchwork magazines and some American ones and has taught throughout Australia.

Influenced by her mathematics teaching background, Cinzia enjoys designing traditional quilts that are based on geometric designs. With perseverance and a desire to explore new directions, she has created many award-winning quilts.

Cinzia enjoys working with color and with no prearranged plan. She has a tendency to incorporate points and curves into her intricate patterns that alternate between two distinct styles: one scrappy and haphazard, the other involving intricate handwork.

It is through her love of handwork that *Raconteur—The Storyteller's Collection* developed. The miniature hexagons, not intended to be finished quickly, were made for her to enjoy stitching and appliquéing by hand. She believes the accuracy and serenity of handwork will always win out over the convenience of machine work.

Cinzia lives in Gerringong, New South Wales, Australia.

Photo by Aimee Kirkham, Oxford-Photography

Visit Cinzia online!

Website: cinziawhite.com

The *Raconteur—The Storyteller's Collection* quilt has won many awards, including:

United Kingdom:

- 2014 UK Nationals—2nd place overall; 1st place theme; 1st place sampler award; 1st place pieced quilt

- 2014 Festival of Quilts, Birmingham, United Kingdom—2nd place Viewer's Choice

Australia:

- 2013 Quilt West—1st place Professional Traditional Quilts

- 2013 Canberra Quilt Show—1st place Bed Quilt Professional

- 2012 SA Festival of Quilts—Retaining the Tradition

- 2012 SA Festival of Quilts—2nd place Professional Bed Quilts

- 2012 NSW Quilt Show—2nd place Viewer's Choice

- Viewer's Choice at numerous local quilt shows

United States:

- Featured in *500 Traditional Quilts*, Lark Books, 2014

- Exhibited by invitation at 2015 Quilt Festival, Houston, Texas; 2016 Quilt Festival, Chicago, Illinois; and numerous other U.S. quilt shows.

- Toured the United States for two years.

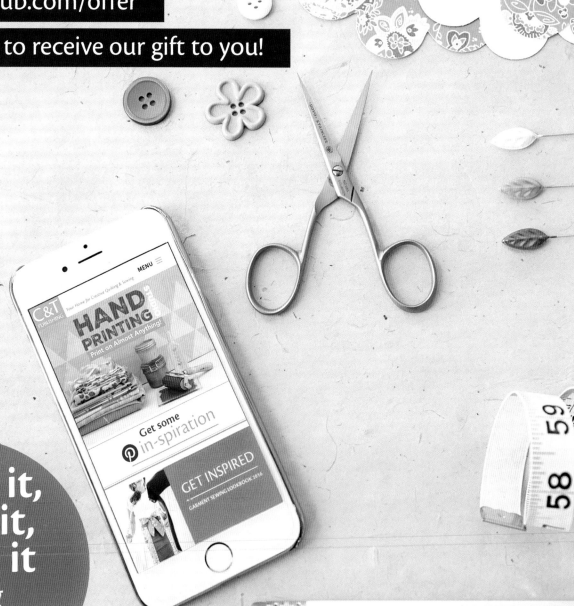

Want even more creative content?

Make it, snap it, share it *using #ctpublishing*